A Fly
Never
Lit

A Fly Never Lit

Delving into characters and events of a past generation in rural Ireland

PJ Cunningham

Ballpoint Press

This book is dedicated to
Sam Rickard (RIP), 'The Man From Next Door'
and his daughter, Eileen Hughes

Published in 2015 by Ballpoint Press
4 Wyndham Park, Bray, Co Wicklow, Republic of Ireland.
Telephone: 00353 86 821 7631
Email: ballpointpress1@gmail.com
Web: www.ballpointpress.ie

ISBN 978-0-9932892-4-8

While every effort has been made to ensure the accuracy of
all information contained in this book, neither the author
nor the publisher accepts liability for any errors or omissions made.

Book design and production by Joe Coyle,
joecoyledesign@gmail.com

Cover photograph: A rural Irish idyll, by iStock/Getty Images

Printed and bound by GraphyCems

Contents

About
The Author

PJ CUNNINGHAM is an author, journalist and publisher who lives with his family in Bray, Co Wicklow but was born and reared on a small farm in Clara, Co Offaly.

His previous book, *The Long Acre*, was shortlisted for the Board Gáis Energy Irish Published Book Of The Year Award in 2014.

He has also written *The Lie Of The Land* (2013) and *A. N. Other*, a book of short stories that focused on rural life as seen through the GAA (2001).

He is married to Rosemary O'Grady and they have five grown-up children.

Preface

THIS collection is the third in a trilogy of memoirs about rural life in Ireland from the latter half of the last century.

It follows on from *The Lie Of The Land*, which was published (2013) and *The Long Acre* which was published last year.

A Fly Never Lit examines the characters and events of a changing Ireland of that time. It is written in stages, from a young boy's observations to his eye-witness accounts as he matures into manhood. We are treated to his personal insights as he watches and listens to the 'ordinary plenty' in the daily life around him.

Largely based on actual events, the stories in the book portray the interaction between families and neighbours within their tightly-knit communities.

Prologue

FIRST, there was the bedroom upstairs with the muffled sound of voices coming from the kitchen below.

Down in the kitchen, there was the stove, the table, the wooden chair and the voices of grown ups chatting to each other.

Out the back door was the yard – a little bit of concrete around the doorstep but mostly muck and dirt down to the cow house and the hayshed.

Out the front, there was the long hallway to the door with its letterbox strapped to it like a schoolbag on a pupil's back.

Beyond the door was the world I grew up in. The road, the neighbours and those few square miles were the extent of Irish country people's universe, only slightly more than half a century ago.

Every time I walked through the front or back door there were human dramas unfurling as people went about their daily work.

Life that time overflowed with the rich vanilla of day to day living. There were Iliads occurring in the next house, the next field or at a stretch the next parish and the tales were recounted at firesides in kitchens like ours every mealtime.

One of the great advantages of being young at that time was the cloak of invisibility it afforded a listener. At least one third of the stories in this collection germinated from conversations I overheard as the unseen observer of six or seven years of age.

Another third are from the time I was aged between seven and 14 when by then I was an occasional contributor to conversations and a continued witness to the performers on their daily stage.

The remainder of the stories I was part of as either a teenager or a young adult.

Consequently the tales in this book are presented as I stepped out the front door and dipped my toes into the stream of stories that flowed around me.

One

A Fly Never Lit

EVERY night the old woman came in to my mother's kitchen with her chipped blue toby jug.

The key was always in our door so she knew to open without knocking and walk down the hall. When she got to the kitchen door, she would always gently tap and then cough to let those inside know who it was.

"Is it yourself?" my mother would say with that welcoming voice of hers that produced warm rays of sunshine in my head every time she inflected her tone in that manner.

"Come in and have a cup of tea," she'd always add.

The old lady always sat on one of the hard wooden chairs, her back perfectly erect, the jug nestling in her lap as she squinted furiously to take in the light under the 60-watt bulb.

My mother felt the world was a dark enough place outside that she insisted on always having light from a strong bulb, though she told my father it was only 40 watt to stop him from giving out.

The old woman lived 50 yards away from our house and preferred to keep a very independent 'distance' from her neighbours. Even when she was the district nurse and was constantly visiting houses around the parish, she kept her own counsel. In particular she held two people at arm's length – her nearest neighbour and her husband.

He was a self-taught engineer long before the time such people got the chance to study the subject at university for years. He had served his time and because he was so good at his job, the owners of the massive jute factory, where over 1,000 people worked in its heyday in our town, had appointed him as head of their entire mechanical and engineering division.

How the nurse and the mechanic originally contrived to come together no one knew – they were the chalk and cheese relationship of their time.

Once, when the husband was due to meet her at an arranged landmark following her trip to her home town to visit relations some six miles away, he had been delayed at work and then set out late in great haste for their rendezvous.

At the other end of the journey, the lady set off in the gathering gloom on her bike using the light of the harvest moon and a flickering bicycle lamp to illuminate her path. Halfway into her journey, she saw in the distance the strong dynamo light of her husband's bike coming in her direction.

Immediately she turned off her own torch, pulled into a gateway behind a tree and waited until her husband pedalled furiously past in a lather of sweat trying to make up for lost time.

She then continued on her way home, knowing her husband would fulfil the barren journey to meet her and have to work out why she wasn't there before making the lonely cycle back on his own.

She had told my mother that story. It didn't reflect well on her in the overall scheme of things but in her view, a person who broke a promise deserved the punishment of having to go on such a fruitless journey. Particularly her husband.

From the time my mother married and had come to live in my father's family home, the old woman had adopted her as someone with whom she was prepared to be friendly. She didn't like her next-door neighbour – a very disciplined and strict woman who had no time for the sort of odd carry on this nurse was known for. "That one is as mad as a March hare," she'd say as she rolled her eyes to my mother in the direction of the old woman's house.

I grew up aware that the nightly knock, and then the cough, would punctuate our evening in as much as the 10 o'clock news on Radio Éireann or the late night tea and currant cake which was our last meal of the day.

There was never any real conversation or sharing of intimacies during those visits. Yet my mother had a grá for the old woman unlike others she might have been friendlier towards but would have had much less time for around the town.

When the old lady's husband died of a massive heart attack on his way home from work one dinner time, the neighbours, including the woman who was her sternest critic, rallied around.

They waked the man in the front room of their two-storey house and my mother took charge of the catering by ensuring there were plenty sandwiches, salads, meats and hot potatoes available in the adjoining kitchen for anyone who came to offer their condolences.

The old lady sat by her husband's head for the duration of the wake, her eyes slightly bloodshot from her tears and the fact that she had taken to wiping them furiously with a grubby handkerchief. She was dignified as she accepted people's sympathies and thanked them for taking the time to pay their respects.

It was the first time I was in the presence of a corpse and I was happy to accept my mother's chosen role for me as her messenger boy. This job entailed bringing in the food and taking out the empty trays and plates to the back kitchen.

Every time I went into the room, it afforded me the opportunity to watch the two – the wife (or new widow) scanning her husband, the corpse, curiously as if he was a new article of furniture.

Once when she left the room to go out for a "breath of fresh air", leaving me alone, I took the opportunity to press my fingers against the dead man's forehead. The unnatural coldness of his skin made me recoil in horror that I had done such a thing.

When she re-entered, she could see that I looked guilty and asked me if I was alright.

"Yes, I'm grand," I lied sheepishly as I swept two of my mother's cups and saucers up off the ledge of a mahogany sideboard and headed for the doorway.

"I hope you didn't touch him because that would be interfering with the dead," she said with such a menace in her voice that I almost dropped the china.

I scurried from the room as quickly as I could, convinced that the woman was a witch, with powers to see through walls.

My mother only smoked when she was upset or worried over something – which meant that she would light up maybe three or four times a week.

The old lady also smoked – didn't everyone at that time – and my mother planted a 10-pack of Players into her black cardigan pocket as I returned to the room. I was glad of the distraction as she seemed to forget totally about me.

In the time before the rosary was recited and the wake ended for the night, the widow smoked all 10 cigarettes, leaving the room looking more like a speakeasy by the time the parish priest arrived to take charge of the religious proceedings.

That night and indeed every other night of that week, my mother brought the milk into the woman's house, had a polite smoke and a chat with her before coming home. I was about six or seven at the time and she would bring me with her whenever she could to use as an 'excuse'.

"I'll go now as I want to put this little man to bed," she'd say as she gathered up her own jug in which she had brought the milk.

This was fine while the old woman was in a grieving period before and after her husband's funeral. However my mother sensed that it was more of an occasion for the old woman to call to our house for the milk and a visit. It would break the monotony of the long evening for her and allow her to have a chat over a cup of tea.

My father was resourceful enough to avoid that hour of the night and would busy himself with chores such as chopping timber in the near shed or cleaning out the cow or calf sheds further down the yard. It was his great escape, whenever he needed it, to excuse himself by saying: 'I don't have the comfort of being able to quit at six (that was the length of the day then) like those people in the factory."

The woman was scary to look at but strangely likeable because she had a warm smile. Her favourite topics of conversation included, my mother claimed, any facet relating to her late husband or his activities.

My mother would nod in agreement, cut a lovely slice

of freshly-baked currant cake, smother it in butter and present it to the woman with her cup.

They would talk, have their nightcap of tea and cake and then a smoke – reluctant on my mother's part – before the old lady would shuffle off to her dark and dreary home just up the road.

As a child, various words and little pieces of her story would stick with me as I played behind the couch in the kitchen. Like the time she told my mother of how and why she avoided her husband on the road. Or much more disturbingly for me when she related how he had burnt out, with a blow torch, a rat in their house from a hole under the stairs.

My mother's skin shivered at the thought, and her jaw dropped in unison with mine as the woman went on: "I wouldn't mind but that was the one creature I ever talked to in the house."

Whatever sort of relationship she had with her man in life, it appeared that his very presence had helped to keep her anchored in some sort of day-to-day reality. Without him, her mind seemed to wander into the realms of confusion.

As the memory of her husband and his death began to fade, she needed to redirect her vitriol elsewhere. Once again my mother gave tacit support in these nightly assaults on the personality and character of another lady, who loomed larger and larger in the conversation as the days went by.

"A real user, that one," she'd say.

"You never said a truer word," agreed my mother.

"A fly never lit," added the neighbour.

"Knew better than to do that," my mother further acquiesced.

Listening to the two women bounce line upon line at each other, I tuned in from my playing with a little lorry and sand to hear several further phrases of deprecation being hurled at this unfortunate other woman's character.

I didn't say anything about what I had heard until after my mother had filled the old woman's jug with milk and accompanied her to the front door.

She would always touch the woman, dressed in black from head to toe, on the shoulder and say: "May God bless and mind you girl and we'll see you in the morning."

She would watch as the woman walked the short journey to her gate where she sometimes spilt some of the milk as she tried to close it behind her.

"Is that woman a witch, Mammy?" I asked, convinced that because she only spoke badly of people and could see through walls that she had some sort of evil powers.

My mother blessed herself at my suggestion, asking me in a stern voice to explain what I meant.

I told her about the corpse and she gave out to me for touching the dead man's forehead.

I kept going despite that rebuke and suggested that the witch was turning her, my mother, into some sort of mean person because they only ever gave out about that other lady.

My mother took a fit of laughing, her shoulders shaking as she did so, before she swept me up in her arms and planted a big kiss on my cheek.

I wriggled free from her grasp and looked at her, totally perplexed by her reaction to what I had said.

"What are you laughing at?" I asked angrily.

Her face became serious as she bent towards me. "Since her husband died, God rest him, the person she gives out about every night, that lady you talked about... well, it's me," she explained, and began laughing again.

"You?" I said incredulously.

"Yes, I'm the one where a fly never lit," said my mother as she put a new cigarette into the coals beneath the fire to light up.

"And do you know what," she chuckled more to herself than to me. "The more she gives out about me, the more I'm beginning to think she might have a point, the poor cratur."

Two

The Man From Next Door

OUR house and farmyard was at the edge of the town beside a housing estate built during the 1940s.

I was a farmer's son and a townie in a sort of contradiction to all the other boys in the school who were either out-and-out townies or rural people.

My mother often said we were the border where town and country met and we were helped by having arguably the largest character ever to live in the town, as a next-door neighbour.

He spent a large part of the last 30 years of his life sitting on our parlour window sill, welcoming and saluting those coming and going along our road.

The sixties were a time when Ireland began to

experience car travel but mostly journeys were undertaken by bicycle or on foot.

My mother loved the man, his sense of humour, his one-line deliveries and his constant commentary about daily life as it passed him by. She said that he was on a stage and she merely provided the audience to his wonderful array of utterances.

This was most likely to occur when sitting on our sill or when he was walking about his own backyard where – out of sight behind a seven-foot wall – he was forever at war with hens and cats and anything else which got under his feet.

As a born and reared countryman, he loved to ask passers-by "how's the work going" when he was on 'sill' duty.

A person coming down the hill on a bike might shout, "hard day on the bog today" to which he would nod in apparent agreement before muttering: "If there was hard work in the bed, that fella would sleep on the floor."

Such was the quality of his aphorisms that often my mother – on a day when his quips overflowed – would relate a plethora of examples as we had our tea in the evening.

My father also had plenty of things in common with him – for one they both smoked the same tobacco in their pipes and would end up borrowing from one another when they were short. Equally important was for one man to produce a light – either a match or a lighter – which was then used to light both Kapp and Petersons.

They were like two Indian chiefs smoking their own peace pipes; often in the evenings they would sit side by side without a word being spoken, just puffing their pipes and watching the world go by.

It was a big world to take in – traffic the far side of the Green Field triangle, traffic coming down from Kilbride and traffic coming up from the town.

He was a man without enemies and worries. Life was full of good reasons to laugh and joke and even when the empty moments arrived and things went wrong for him, he seemed to always find a way to sway the hand of providence to work in his favour.

No matter what the situation was, he had the gift to handle it with aplomb. I saw him defusing a row at a toss pit by reminding one of the adversaries how his father would curse the pennies at such infantile behaviour. The man shut up, the coins fell in his favour and he looked at the aggravated man with a disarming smile as if to say: "Learn from that."

Equally, he had a gift to elevate, even enrich, sombre occasions. The death of my granny was the first time the grim reaper had knocked directly at our door in my lifetime. My father's sister, my godmother, was distraught at the loss of her mother, who was her soul mate and confidante. As a very religious woman she was sure of where her mother was headed but it couldn't take from the heavy sorrow in her heart.

Until he arrived.

Unlike everyone else who had held her hand, hugged her quietly and spoken their condolences into her ear, our neighbour walked into the room where my granny was laid out in the bed and ignoring my aunt and the others who were seated in hard chairs along the wall, began addressing the corpse as if she was still alive.

"Yea," he repeated a few times as he regarded her face, shrivelled slightly in death.

"I hear you are already a hit up there," he said pointing at the ceiling. With those few words, he had caught the full attention of my aunt and the other women.

"Yea," he went on again. "The lad on the gate welcomed you in and said you were one in a million. And sent you straight up to the man Himself."

He got a little emotional at what he was saying, and rubbed his bulging eyes with a tatty handkerchief that had seen better days.

"Mind now," he stressed, "while you're so close to Himself, be sure to get excuses in for people you know who might have the odd failing like myself when it's my turn to go. Do you hear now? Good. Because you know me better than anyone, I'll be counting on that."

Having lived next door to my Granny for years, he still remained close to her when she moved out of our house to another dwelling a few hundred yards up the

THE MAN FROM NEXT DOOR

road. That occurred after her daughter and my uncle and my father and mother had married in a double wedding. Up to my granny's relocation, our neighbour had built a bond with her similar, I think, to the one my mother would later develop with him.

I was very young at the time and was looking in to the bedroom where he had just completed his impromptu eulogy to my granny. Mostly I was captivated by the reaction of my aunt as he undertook his address to the dead. She went from sadness, virtual hopelessness and despair to something approaching joy both at what he said and the way he said it.

It is an image that has stayed with me down the years and the older I get the more I realise that really he was addressing the living left behind in that chamber of death.

My aunt led him down to the kitchen, poured him a drink and appeared to be walking on air as they both spoke fondly about my granny. Quite simply the man had the gift to transform and I don't think my aunt cried a tear either at the wake or during the funeral after his simple yet profound farewell.

Without ever trying to be it, he was the centre of attention wherever he was. For years he worked on the roads. The foreman there admitted that when our neighbour was around, there was far less work done but the consolation for him was that he was supervising a happier crew. And like all good bosses he knew that his life was much easier in such circumstances.

His great passion in life was dogs – greyhounds were in his blood. The dog track owners also loved to have him around and treated him well. They wanted him to succeed because any night he was at the dogs, he would engage punters and make them feel like he was giving them the inside track.

Our town had a long and strong history of people going in groups over to Aintree for the Grand National. Normally a publican would arrange the travel for some of his customers and himself. Mostly they were happy to go once our neighbour went too. It took a lot of money to get over and back not to mention having sufficient largesse for drink and gambling there as well.

For a man with a large family and not blessed with a big paying job, he never let a lack of money get in his way. Every street corner provided him with the possibility of raising a shilling.

Like the time the group went to Liverpool and lost their bearings and their shirts on the horses. As they woke up late in their lodgings around the city centre on the following morning, they could find no place open for Sunday Mass.

Seeing the bishop's palace, the neighbour approached the door with a knock that serendipitously the bishop himself answered. Explaining the predicament of his group having to face a sailing across the Irish Sea in the afternoon with the fear of mortal sin and eternal damnation ringing in their ears, he asked the "Father" if it would be possible to get a Mass said.

The bishop was taken by the manner and demeanour of the likeable Irishman and said if the group came back in half an hour, he would personally say a Mass for them.

By the time he had told his own group of the service he had just arranged, several other Irish men had heard of the special Mass and asked if they could tag along. He welcomed them all to follow him so that by the time the bishop opened the door once more, he was surprised to see the numbers that filtered into the pews in the nearby chapel.

At the conclusion of the ceremony as the bishop made his way from the altar into the vestry, our neighbour told the congregation how privileged and indebted they should be that a priest would take the time to look after them. He then put a half-crown into his own hat and passed it to one of his group, directing him to collect from all the others before they dispersed.

The congregation followed his example; they dug as deeply as they could under the circumstances and by the time the hat had done the rounds, it was indeed well nourished with a mixture of English and Irish coins.

Accepting that the Mass had taken place through his own sense of entrepreneurship and the bishop's willingness to take on such a task, he entered the vestry and unloaded the contents in front of his lordship. He pushed a larger portion of the money in the bishop's direction and swept up the rest into his own two hands, expertly trousering it in one movement.

"Everyone happy?" he asked rhetorically.

The bishop smiled and bowed, enriched financially and spiritually by a man who never saw a problem in life, only a solution.

It could be argued the ultimate judgement of a man is not how he lives but how he dies.

In time even this great epicurean had to face the fact that he could not live forever. The empty window sill made him conspicuous by his absence, leading people to ask where he was as they passed by.

The power had initially begun to desert his stuttering legs and despite constant attention from the medical services, it became clear that he would not see out another winter.

There was sadness as the word spread that this larger than life player would no longer tread his public stage again. Yet his closing scene in life still managed to raise a smile throughout the town before his final curtain fell.

With the family having come from far and wide to be around him in his last hours, he asked that a particular priest – the son of one of his best friends in life – should be summoned to his bedside.

Upon his arrival the children and their families were sent to the back kitchen out of earshot. After about half an hour, the man of the cloth emerged from the downstairs bedroom to tell the gathering that they were now required to go back inside.

Although weak in voice and body, the dying man's message was clear: "This priest has made me very happy now as I set out on the journey across the great divide. I want to thank him for that and for the peace I now feel."

Then nodding towards an empty sock he had on a locker beside the bed, he told them, his own flesh and blood, to show their appreciation by having a whip-around. "I don't want to hear the sound of coppers or silver either," he emphasised.

His family, obviously emotional in such circumstances, were only too happy to acquiesce with his final demand – and made a substantial silent collection into his sock.

When they were finished, he lifted himself up slightly on the pillow and with the loudest whisper left in his body, ordered: "You can all leave Father and myself alone again."

After they had filed out, wiping back tears at what they had just witnessed, the priest closed the door and looked back into the bedroom.

He noticed that while our neighbour was certainly indisposed and visibly ailing from the man he knew all his life, the twinkle was still present in his eye.

The sick man nodded towards the sock: "For you," he said.

The priest began to gently protest when he was

arrested from that course by the raising of a hand from the man in the bed which demanded immediate silence.

"I said it's yours," he declared.

Then as an afterthought, he added: "I won't be insulted if you leave a few quid in the sock... sure a man never knows when he might need something to be going on with."

He then closed his eyes, smiled and went on his last journey beyond his little room to where I have no doubt my granny, among others, had already smoothed the way for his safe delivery through and beyond the pearly gates.

Three

A Miracle At Christmas

IT was Christmas Eve morning and for once snow had fallen, making the house, the yard and the fields around look like the picture postcards that had arrived offering seasonal greetings through our letterbox for the previous few weeks.

The sound of squirting milk from the udder of a cow my father was milking in the cowshed acted as a gentle drumroll of calm as the animals chewed on the hay I had earlier thrown into their mangers.

We worked in unison; my father milking, my brother spreading the straw bedding and I by bringing in the forks of hay.

The snow acted as a silencer on the earth except for the strange squish it made under my feet as I walked across the yard to the hayshed. For someone who had a short but very focused list for Santa Claus or Santie as we called him – two guns, two pouches and a cowboy hat – life less than 24 hours away from delivery could not have been much better.

My brother was three years older and efforts to engage him in talks about Santie had changed over the previous year or so – he seemed indifferent to the fact that the man would bring him a shirt and tie as well as a book. Seemed to me like he was seriously short-changed but he appeared happy enough in an offhand sort of way.

The cows were milked only once a day at that time of year – and even then, it was quarts rather than gallons that my father was getting from them. Among the four still lactating, we had enough for our own house and the six houses around the holding to which we delivered either a pint or a quart of milk a day.

His worry though was for the fifth cow in the shed – she had gone down a few days beforehand and was unable to get up on her four legs to stand by herself.

She was still able to eat the hay and turnips we put in front of her but we also had to bring buckets of water and hold them under her head so that she could drink and keep her alive.

When he had finished milking, my father went over to where she was lying down and tried to encourage her to stand.

"Good girl, get up," he coaxed as he slapped her

gently on the back to try to invigorate action into her bones.

Over our breakfast that morning, the snow continued to fall. My father said he hoped it would stop as otherwise we would have to give extra fodder out to the cattle and sheep in the fields. "Snow is a divil on livestock. The sooner it turns to slush the better."

It left me feeling guilty to hope we would have a white Christmas but already there were children out on the roads making a snowman. Their squeals of delight could be heard far away, increasing my yearning to join them.

"Go on," my mother said, "the two of ye might as well have a bit of fun while it's here. Leave the worrying about livestock to me and your father."

Within minutes, we were throwing snowballs and when those bouts ceased, we gathered fleeces of snow to add to the size of the snowman.

The cold from the snow was fierce, it burnt into my fingers as if they were held over flames. I flapped my arms across my body to try to warm them but it was no use. I had to run back to the house and open the grate of the fire to allow a thawing process to begin.

My brother stayed on outside with his friends and I must have become invisible in the kitchen as my parents began to talk about the cow.

"Don't let it spoil Christmas," urged my mother.

"I won't," my father said. "All I'm saying is that I've

never seen a cow that went down on its haunches, ever get back up again."

The day closed in early and the white blankets across the ground grew in thickness.

We stocked up with extra logs for the fire and my father brought in a few more buckets of turf as my mother had let it be known she would light a second fire – in the parlour.

She did this just as the day darkened prematurely and at the same time turned on the lights on the Christmas tree for the first time. The world was magical through that evening; the blinking lights at the end of the room, the flickering tongues of flame in the fireplace and the flutter of falling snow outside the window gave the night a perfect backdrop to welcome Santa Claus down our chimney.

It was a wrench to go into the kitchen for supper but my mother would never dream of serving food in the parlour – except between Christmas Day and Little Christmas and on our birthdays.

It was her ritual and she had made it ours.

She also revealed later that I was now a big enough 'maneen,' as she called me, for us all to go to midnight mass that year.

It meant having to be in the chapel by 11 o'clock as the pews filled up quickly and it was no joke to have to stand at the very back for such a long ceremony. We waited for my aunt and her family who my mother said would also be going with us, but they were late.

My father was treading uneasily from one foot to the other as he scanned the road from the doorway to see if they were approaching.

"If they don't come soon, we'll have to stand," he shouted back into my mother.

"They'll be here in a minute," she responded as she put her gloves on at the hallstand mirror, having secured the knot on her yellow headscarf tightly under her chin.

We heard the chatter of my cousins before we saw them at the doorway.

"Always late," said my mother with a chuckle as her sister burst through the doorway and headed for the toilet.

"Better late than never," she answered as she stepped on the butt-end of her cigarette.

We managed to get two half pews for the two families in the church. I sat with my brother and cousins and the adults sat in the row behind us.

The service was different with so much music and singing accompanying the usual domination of the Latin mass. My brother was an altar boy and could say things in Latin that sounded great. "Suscipio domini sacrificio de manibus tuum," he could recite and I would marvel at how clever he sound.

A man ahead of us smelled of drink and was interspersing the odd dry wretch with singing loudly through the many carols. I turned around to my mother, who pulled a face of disapproval at his antics.

She hated people who drank too much and this man obviously fitted that bill. I too detested the smell of stale porter that wafted back from him every time he opened his mouth. My main worry was that if he threw up, both my mother and brother would react by getting sick as well. They both had delicate constitutions.

The concelebrated mass was better than the normal one I used to go to. Even the large crowd receiving Holy Communion was no problem because there were five priests on the altar and three gave out the hosts in the centre aisle with the others looking after those receiving on the two side aisles.

Outside afterwards, it was cold and fresh but also exciting and invigorating to be up at half one in the morning and to see the snow still falling.

The adults told my cousins and us that we better get to sleep as soon as we got home or Santie would leave us nothing until next year.

I knew my mother would know when the right time was to go to bed so I'd no worries on that score. By the time we got to the house, our cheeks were aglow with the sting of the cold night air.

"Rough weather on cattle," my father remarked as he came back in from the scullery with a cup of water to wash his mouth out after receiving.

My aunt had lit her Goldflake from the ashes and nodded in agreement as she inhaled her first pull of the cigarette.

My mother was busy putting rashers and sausages on the pan and got me to move behind my aunt to "liven up the fire."

Neighbours and friends were invited to join with us in the eating of this post midnight fry.

My mother took out a bale of briquettes from under the stairs that she kept for special occasions and used them to top up the stove. We wanted to move into the parlour but she said lighting the fire there earlier was just to get the chill out of the chimney for Christmas Day.

"It's a special room if we use it on special occasions only," she reasoned.

The crowded kitchen and the quality of heat emanating from the rayburn meant we had to open the door into the hallway to let in fresh air. I sat on a little stool in the corner where I could put my head against the warm wall. Despite my best efforts to stay awake, sleep was winning the battle with my eyes.

The noise of conversation and spitting logs faded from my hearing as I lost the struggle and fell asleep. The next thing I could recall was being tucked into bed and the light being put out.

From below the hum of chat was still audible but only until my mother closed the door behind her on the way out of my room.

When I woke up, I knew by the light of the day that it was late. I jumped from the bed when I remembered it was Christmas morning.

Santie had been here.

My parents and brother were in the middle of their breakfast when I opened the door into the kitchen.

They looked at me and smiled as I came in with eyes still fighting to see clearly.

"Sleepy head," said my mother as she ran her hand through my hair.

"Did Santie come?" I asked.

"I think I heard him about six o'clock," said my father.

Bowing to my impatience, they left their half-eaten breakfast to accompany me into the parlour.

The tradition was that the youngest – me – opened the door.

There, sitting on the mat in front of the fireplace, were our presents. He had delivered as promised with the cowboy rigout. I was so happy that I couldn't wait to put them on and go down the yard to start shooting.

I walked down the snow-covered haggard with my father. The snow had stopped falling but the air was bitter and the sky looked pregnant with dark, distended clouds that might contain more fallout.

My father opened the cowshed door and immediately the animals rose to their feet in anticipation of being fed.

The sick one was at the far end and we watched intently as she tried to get her legs under her. She rocked backwards and forwards without managing to hold a steady gait.

"I've never seen one get back up," my father repeated exactly as he had said to my mother in the kitchen the previous day.

"Never."

As he spoke, the animal made a renewed effort to raise herself up from the concrete floor that my brother had covered the previous evening with thick layers of straw to keep her warm for the nighttime.

As we watched from the doorway, she managed to get her four legs under her but like the drunk man in front of us at midnight mass, she swayed from side to side on unsteady pins.

The two of us held our breaths. My father blessed himself three times in rapid succession. Immediately, I followed suit.

I was aware then that – with the snow falling, the experience of midnight mass, the cowboy set present from Santie – if she could stay standing up now, it would be the most miraculous Christmas we would ever have as a family.

Four

The Shoes Of The Fisherman

O N the bank of the 'Big River' his personality changed.

He had led us from our home full of joy and laughter, talking about people and things from his past as if they were props in the jokes he was about to tell.

Even his breathing was louder than any I had ever heard and his laughter went through gears as an initial high shriek was followed on by eddies of chesty howls.

My mother said my uncle – my father's brother – was the "larger than life" one in the family.

From the moment he arrived at our house he was a barrel of fun and games – the serious stuff he said he had lumped on his older brother – my father's – shoulders.

He was the boy who didn't stay on the farm and instead turned his considerable engineering gifts to run his own mechanical, plumbing and roofing business in Dublin.

While most people spoke of Dublin from street level, he was something of a living caped crusader – always viewing the city from its rooftops.

He had worked on South Circular Road church opposite where he lived, as well as all the hospitals and both Christchurch and St Patrick's Cathedral. Up there he said there was plenty of work to be done. If the slates weren't broken when he got up there, by the time he had finished walking across the various roofs, there was enough work to keep him going for weeks on end. That was the joke he told against himself because while my father would often give out about him on many levels, he would make a point of saying that my uncle was as honest as the day was long.

He would hardly be out our front door when my father explained to us how he was a great craftsman but "a lousy businessman."

"Sure his wife has to go and collect the money because he wouldn't ask for it himself."

Still, this couldn't dim the light he shone into our lives. He was this great man mountain who threw us skywards until we hit the ceiling in our kitchen or put our little legs dangling either side of his neck as we sat on his shoulders crossing the 'Little River' which ran through our fields.

The Sunday morning rain had cleared into a fresh summer's afternoon when he arrived at our door.

After his preferred refreshment of coffee and scones – my mother had to send me flying down to the shops for the coffee – he made a pronouncement that nearly burst the heart in my chest with excitement.

"Let's go for an evening's fishing in the 'Big River,'" he said to my brother and I.

My mother's eyes rolled in horror; the thought of water was enough to kick off fears in her head of the two of us being drowned.

He picked up on her hesitant response by joking: "Bring your top-boots in case you need to save me if I fall in."

She smiled at him as she bent under the table to get our wellingtons ready for the expedition. She encouraged my father to go with us, knowing that if he did she would have no need to worry.

He sniggered, saying it was alright for the idle rich to go shooting or fishing but poor people like himself were tied to the grind seven days a week. This didn't please our mother but she knew once he had made his decision, he couldn't be persuaded to change.

As she waved goodbye to us outside the house, her left hand went up to her mouth and she used her right across her forehead as a shield against the sun rays to follow the progress of the car down the road as far as the chapel. When we turned right at the junction we were out of her sight and on the main road to the 'Big River.'

At the shop halfway on the journey, he stopped to say hello "to an old squeeze" and bought us two ice creams.

When we got to the bridge over the 'Big River', we pulled into a grass margin just beyond it and got out of the car.

My uncle's eyes scanned the ditch and he told us we'd make fishing rods out of the hazel tree branches. He cut two long rods, then pared the bark off them with his penknife before returning to the boot of the car. He took out a spool of fishing line and a number of hooks which he had placed in an empty black shoe-polish tin.

He put the items in his jacket pocket, took up the newly whittled rods and then signalled to us to follow him over the stile and down the path along the winding river. After walking for about five minutes, he took the tackle out of his coat which he then spread on the grass.

"That's our base, lads" he said as we knelt on it and he began his work.

He was so immersed – tying the wire to the rod – that he hardly spoke for 10 minutes. Then he felt the weight and the flexibility of the first rod as he made several pretend casts in the direction of the gurgling water. Each time, he adjusted slightly the knots he had tied at the top of the stick in his search for a better balance.

In the quiet that had descended on our afternoon, my attention was drawn to how his big hands and fingers could produce such neat and precise finishing to what he was assembling. This was particularly the case when he wed the hooks from the polish tin with the line that hung from the pole.

"Perfect," he said quietly to himself as he saw how the hook anchored the wire.

"Time to find the worms, lads," he added. "There'll be no bites without the worms to attract them."

He led us over to a spot where the lush grass of the field had come up against the stony soil close to the headland. We sourced several wiggly earthworms almost immediately which my uncle put into the polish tin before putting the lid back on.

As we regrouped at the river, he inched to the side of the water before casting into the middle of the stream.

"You take turns," he instructed us as he pointed at the remaining homemade rod on the bank. My brother lifted up the stick, took a worm out of the tin and impaled it on the hook just as my uncle had done moments before.

His first attempt to cast off saw the worm and the hook go their separate ways – my uncle was so engrossed in his own pursuit of fish that he didn't notice.

The next time we tried, we pulled the worm into three parts and put the different pieces on the hook, one after the other. When he tried the casting with this new method, the worm stayed on.

My uncle was totally concentrated on the flowing water and what lay beneath to the extent that we were afraid to break the silence by talking.

The fishing had brought new, unspoken ground rules and we were abiding by them.

I pointed to the rod to signal that I wanted a turn but my brother ignored me as he felt a tug at the other end of the line.

He pulled hard at the invisible opponent but the disappointment of 'catching' only a big river weed from the bed of the waterway was palpable.

We then put on another worm and my brother handed me the reins. At last, it was my turn.

My initial cast-off caught a furze bush behind where I stood which resulted in the two of us spending several minutes trying to extricate our line and hook from the bushes.

The next time I was mindful to jerk the line in the direction of the water rather than cast it. This resulted in it falling perilously close to the near side of the bank, but with my brother being taller and having a longer reach, he came to my aid by helping to negotiate it out closer to midstream.

I tried to copy my uncle's unconscious rhythm of working the rod by weaving and flipping it against the water as it flowed in the direction away from the bridge.

Zoning in on the area of my line just above the water, I visualised the lower end of the hook and worm and wondered if it was close to a fish mouth of any persuasion.

I stood there with my two arms working to keep the line free to drift with the water, my legs stuttered on the bank while I tried to wriggle the line sideways to make the worm's movement interesting to a passing fish.

Minute upon minute passed without success and although the sun had gone further down on the sky out west bringing a cooler chill around us, my body was pumping with the effort I was putting in to get that elusive bite.

Ten yards downstream I noticed my uncle had entered the river close to the top of his boots. He had become part of the surroundings and moved in time with the wind above him and waters flowing in and around him.

I had never seen him so content. For a man who needed to talk and joke to breathe, it was now obvious even to an eight year old like me that he needed the hush of this riverbank even more.

I knew at that moment that we would catch no fish that day and part of me was disappointed. My uncle had introduced the two of us to something on that riverbank which was beyond the ephemeral moments of catching a fish or recounting others that got away. He had brought us to a new experience and invited us into a world we didn't know existed... we were following in the shoes of the fisherman.

Five

The Circus Clown

BANG, bang, bang.

The sound of hammering echoed like gunshots outside my front-room window; it drifted up from the big triangular green field down below that acted as the town's play-pen.

The cacophonic rhythm punctuated the early morning singing of the birds, standing like sentinels on the four trees outside our house.

It took a few more seconds for me to realise that the circus was in town. I barely remembered the last time it had visited but there was no mistaking the buzz that was coming from the field as the workers went about erecting the tent.

Boys and girls making their way to school watched

as the men worked furiously in the arena.

The workers wielding the sledgehammers had already dressed down in the early April chill to their thick vests at the constant labouring task of driving iron spikes deep into the ground. These would act as anchors for the guy ropes to secure the Big Top for the audiences who would visit it over that weekend before it would again be dismantled and moved on to the next town.

The whole operation was undertaken with ant-like precision and for us as children, it was exhilarating to watch.

In the background, the elephants, the buffaloes and the horses were being led from the vehicles in which they had been transported down ramps and onto the grass. Only the lions were being left caged in their quarters, though they were prowling up and down their enclaves as if they sensed an occasion where they could make their escape.

The fact that the children had to be in school prevented us all from staying and watching this mesmeric scene unfolding in front of our eyes. Someone said we had 10 minutes to run the mile or we would all be late. Like a herd of stampeding rhino, we bolted off as one, away from the allure of the circus. We ran down the main street of the town, our bags shaking on our backs as we sped along with the intention of being in before the monk entered our classroom.

Our schoolteacher was kindly and when we told him

why we were all perspiring so much, he responded by instructing us that we could spend the morning writing a story about the circus. He asked us how many of us would go to the matinée the following day – Saturday – and we didn't know what a matinée was.

So he explained there would be a show for children in the afternoon which would cost less than if we went with the adults at nighttime. Some people put up their hands straight away, others like myself were perplexed as we wondered if it would cost our parents too much money.

By the time we had finished school that afternoon and returned excitedly to the circus site, it had been totally transformed into a mobile village in the middle of the town. On one side, there were caravans like a row of terraced houses with washing lines jutting out from the side.

Across to the other side of the Big Top was the animal area and already the distinct smell of dung permeated from their enclosure and wafted out as far as the road.

A man on a stepladder was hammering posters absent-mindedly along an entrance corridor announcing the 'Live and Exclusive Big Top Spectacular' taking place in the town later that evening, twice on the Saturday and twice on the Sunday.

He cursed under his breath when the cigarette he was holding in his mouth fell as he hammered in the nail at the top of the final poster.

"Holy Jesus Christ," he roared as the butt-end burnt his chest in his haste to sweep it away from his clothing.

He had curly red hair and the burn on his white skin looked raw. He spat on his hand and rubbed the spittle into the wound while at the same time using his other hand to fan his skin with his straw hat.

When he took time to look up, he saw us – a group with our schoolbags on our backs – just staring at him.

He glowered at us, made as if he was about to utter some profanity before shrugging his shoulders, picking up his ladder and walking into the circus tent.

Later that afternoon, my father arrived home with a jog of hay for the calves and cows that were still being kept in sheds because the growing season was late that year. The hay he brought was from a rick he kept on our land a mile away. It was now needed as we had run out of the feed in the hayshed at home.

Within minutes of arriving into the yard, two men from the circus walked across from the Green Field and into our backyard.

"Excuse me, sir," said the smaller man in a strong voice. "Do you mind if we come in?"

My father squinted from inside the hayshed where he had backed the mare and cart and beckoned at the pair to advance towards him.

It was then I noticed that the other man was the person who had burnt himself with a cigarette earlier on my way home from school.

The smaller man introduced himself as the owner of the circus and asked my father if it would be possible to buy hay and straw for his elephants, lions, buffaloes and horses.

"We normally have a supplier for fodder but because of the long winter, the man has run out," he explained.

My father told him that the hay was scarce enough that year but he would oblige him and would also give him as many bales of straw as he wanted.

"I don't want to gild the lily but could we also trouble you for water as we have to go down the town to get it in containers," the circus leader enquired.

Our house was only a short distance away from where his animals were caged so it made sense for him to source an alternate supply if he could find it.

My father was a man who knew when he had an adversary in a corner on a commercial footing but for some reason he didn't appear too pushed to drive home that advantage.

That seemed to endear him to the owner who ended up agreeing a £5 fee for two loads of straw from the horse and cart and one jog of hay.

That evening as we ate our supper, the only topic of conversation was circus-related. My mother told my father it was daylight robbery to take a five-pound note for a few wisps of hay but my father said he could have held out for more because he had him over a barrel.

"And besides I've given him all the straw he wants and the water is a Godsend for them as well."

No sooner had the words come out of his mouth than we were all startled by a loud knocking on the door.

For a moment we froze before my father pushed back his chair and went out into the hall.

The voice was unfamiliar; but when I peered out from the kitchen doorway down the hallway, I could see it was the ginger man who burnt himself that was standing in the doorway.

"The boss sent me over," he began. "He said to thank you for the fodder and to give you these tickets for your children and yourselves for the matinée tomorrow."

My father thanked him profusely and as they continued to stand on either side of the doorstep, he belatedly asked him in for a cup of tea. The man declined graciously and backed away from the door out into the cover of the night.

The four tickets had the word 'complimentary' stamped across them. I didn't know what that meant but I knew for sure that we would all go to the circus – something even better than winning the Sweeps in my eyes.

My father couldn't go on the following day so my mother said I could bring my friend from next door with me and my brother instead. That made the whole experience even more rewarding as my friend's mother gave us money to buy ice cream at the interval.

The show was laden with interest – the lion tamer was amazing; the trapeze artists had us looking up as they performed death-defying leaps and jumps as tarzan-like, they traversed the podium on ropes without any nets underneath in the event of a fall.

After so much fear in one afternoon, the clowns came on and had the crowd calling for more. The ginger haired man was the lead clown and he began by pretending to be drunk and saying he was going into bed to go to sleep. On the podium was a tent and as he got ready he lit a candle and put it in a bottle to hold it upright.

'Nightie, night, childee," he said exaggeratedly to us and we just knew he would set fire to his tent before long.

The next we saw of him, he was running out of the room and around the main ring with his backside on fire. He desperately tried to put out his rear by sitting in a bucket of water. Then his posterior became stuck and we laughed as he tripped himself up trying to pull the bucket away.

"Could someone help me, childee?" he asked us. I put my hand up but before I could move, he had picked my friend who had already vaulted the outside of the ring perimeter and was now the main attraction in the centre of the stage.

I felt jealous that the man who had given us the tickets had picked my friend ahead of me but almost immediately was glad that I wasn't under the spotlight.

The clown had long, long pointy shoes on and kept kicking my friend up the backside as ostensibly he had him trying to pull the bucket off his. Then when my friend tried to walk away, he tripped him – much to the delight of the audience.

I was mortified because I could see my friend was about to cry and after my initial feeling of envy, I now felt very protective of him.

The clown then offered to lift him up but as he did, he suddenly took his hand away forcing my friend to fall on his back.

The clown laughed out at the crowd who returned his laughter. The owner, who was also the MC, saw my friend was near to crying and took the microphone into his hand.

"Boys and girls, a big hand for the little boy, he's been a good sport."

He then took a packet of sweets out of his pocket and thrust them into my friend's hands.

I thought that the little man was great to do that as my friend came back with something to show for his stint as the butt of the clown's jokes.

After the show my mother brought my brother and I to my friend's house. She whispered to his mother about the incident with the clown and then out loud said: "He was a great lad and the owner gave him sweets for being so good."

My friend smiled but I could see he knew my mother was only being nice; he had felt humiliated and no sweets would make that go away.

By the time the main show was due to go on at

8pm, the humming of the circus's own generator dispelled the dark of the night with eight high-powered lamps lighting up the entrance to and inside the Big Top itself.

By then my friend and I were back out on the Green Field watching as hundreds of people queued to get their tickets into the night show.

When the show started, we could hear it plainly outside of the canvas of the Big Top. Having attended the matinée, it was easy to imagine what was happening as the MC roared: "Ladies and gentlemen, from Budapest in Hungary, the amazing high-flying trapeze artists."

The clown segment in the show was the same but this time he got a grown-up to be his fall guy. From the shrieking of the crowd, we both knew the man was going through the same tried and trusted tricks to get the audience to laugh.

The interval was long and afterwards, there was much more time devoted to the elephants and the horses and the blast of brass section music filled the night air outside.

"Let's see if we can sneak in," my friend suggested. "It is dark around the back and we could get under the canvas and watch from behind the seats."

We checked to be sure the coast was clear before stealing around by the caravans away from the entrance to the circus.

My friend was more adroit than I and with a few

wiggles had squeezed underneath the canvas to get inside.

I made an attempt to do as he did but found myself stuck half way in and half way out. As I turned my body in an attempt to wriggle my way in, I got a ferocious kick on the part of my back that was still sticking out of the canvas.

I was winded but a sixth sense told me that unless I moved immediately there would be another boot coming at me very soon. Summoning up all the strength I could muster, I arched myself back out while at the same time turning quickly away from the direction that I had been kicked.

As I did so, the second kick came in but not expecting such a sudden movement from me, it missed the target. Unable to adjust his stance quickly enough, the kicker became unbalanced and fell over, winding himself against an iron spike. I felt a huge pang of guilt until I saw in the half-light that it was the clown who had kicked me.

He shook his head in apparent disbelief.

"Holy Jesus Christ," he shrieked for the second time in a few days as he gasped for full breath.

By this time my friend had become aware of the commotion and was back out at my side.

"What happened?" he asked as he tried to make sense of a clown on the ground holding his back and wheezing.

"He fell over trying to kick me," I said ashamed

that he had actually made contact and its effect was still causing me considerable pain in my lower back.

The clown tried to stand up but only managed to stagger against the side of the Big Top.

"Nightie night childee yourself," my friend spat at the man who was still swaying on his feet.

"Let's go," he said to me. "We've had enough of that clown for one day."

Six

The Great Land Divide

WHILE John B Keane's *The Field* was an extreme example of how highly emotive a plot of land could be, it was also indicative of the importance in which it was held.

The poet Patrick Kavanagh had a few immortal lines in his poem Epic – "Who owned that half a rood of rock, a no-man's land surrounded by our pitchfork-armed claims."

Land is, or at least was, worth fighting for and people who opposed you in fighting for that right could suffer everlasting pain.

"I heard the Duffys shouting 'Damn your soul'" was indicative of the culture that if you interfered with a man's (women didn't get a look in then) parcel of land, the consequences could reach a higher court in heaven for adjudication.

Amidst all this turmoil over roods and acres, the Land Commission managed to transfer thousands upon thousands of acres during its 110 years of operation in Ireland up to 1992 when it ceased to exist.

Although introduced in the last decades of British rule (1882), it sought to give as many people as possible 22-acre holdings which were back then deemed sufficient for a man to sustain his family. Like everything else, there was method in their madness. In keeping the new holdings to such a size, it meant those small farmers would have to sell on most of their young livestock to larger landowners. This would guarantee them a supply line of raw material on which they could make the real financial killing when they in turn sold them.

Although the Commission remarkably managed to take land off one owner and transfer to another without any notable degree of bloodshed or proper compensation – they paid in virtually worthless land bonds – the body was regarded with suspicion and a slight fear by ordinary rural folk.

Indeed many were wary of how it operated and who benefitted, often to cries of skullduggery and favouritism.

The Commission was still very active in the mid-sixties and when a Protestant landowner died in our part of the world, his estate was taken over by the government body for redistribution. It was a holding between a hundred and two hundred statute acres and was within a quarter of a mile of our lands – or more precisely near to where the bulk of our scattered holding was located.

For farm and rural families, the dishing out of such land was akin to winning or being in the running to win the lottery nowadays. A small holding such as ours could be transformed into a 'good farm' with the addition of an extra 20 or 30 acres.

Around us, farmers large and small were optimistic that they would benefit from the Commission's decision to grant them extra acreage.

The division of the land became a hot topic of conversation after and sometimes during mass or wherever two farmers sat or walked side by side.

My father said very little on the whole issue – he had a distrust of most government agencies, feeling from experience in his lifetime that politics came before fairness or justice.

Yet, this time around he had, at least on the face of it, a strong case just like the other farmers around him. There seemed to be enough land for all of them to get a slice and still be relatively happy should the Commission so decide.

Officials paid visits to homes and to the property up for division and every sighting was a cause of renewed excitement as to when the final word would be made and announced.

In our house we never got so far as to ask for intercession from on-high but it always cropped up in conversation after the rosary when the late tea and currant bread were served.

"Knowing our luck, we'll be passed over," my father said more than once, much to the chagrin of my mother.

"Well if people hear you talking like that, you're bound to be right," she remarked.

My aunt, who was a farmer and a good judge, said there was no earthly reason why we shouldn't get a leg up in life.

"Another few acres would give you the chance to expand herd numbers and make farming worthwhile," she said.

She was right because on the 52 Irish acres we possessed, life was a hand to mouth subsistence. Not quite 'live horse and get grass' but not too much of a step up from that either.

In the weeks leading up to the announcement, people talking about the likely winners of the Commission's largesse had become very technical, speaking about family size, age profile and other criteria that might be used in the final judgement.

My father was about 60 at the time and with two sons, many felt that while there were others with small holdings and larger families, none was as local with their land as we were. They considered this a massive plus, though he himself seemed less enthused.

Like Kavanagh's poem I lived when great events such

as the carving up of that estate was decided and I can remember the sense of hope that it engendered in all of us.

Unfortunately to this day, I can see my father's face, loaded with disappointment and also feel my mother's tears when he came home one evening to tell us that we hadn't made the cut in the divide.

"Who got it?" asked my mother, shaking her head when she heard some of the names and nodding in acceptance at the ones she deemed worthy to get more land.

To everybody who discussed the outcome over the subsequent days, we became the 'hard luck story' of the Land Commission's decision.

People showed genuine regret when speaking to my mother down the town or stopping my father on the pony and cart as he made his way from our house down to the land in Woodfield.

He was gracious in defeat. "We got by before without it..." he'd say without finishing the sentence. It became his stock reply to those bringing up the subject.

I learned a lot about life watching him during those days and the way he handled the disappointment he so obviously felt.

Instead of dwelling on his own misfortune, he would subtly turn the story around to someone who had got an allotment and simply say: "You know I'm nearly as happy for him getting it as if I got it myself."

His greatest disappointment only came out some

days later when I overheard him talking to my mother in the kitchen.

"That puts an end to either of the lads ever making a go of farming," he said. "With the sort of parcels that were given out, I'd have said there was hope a farm that size could support one of them making a living. But not now."

My mother agreed, adding that farming was the "last shift anyway" and "all you got was hardship out of land."

"The next generation will be better off holding pens in their hands than shovels," she declared in a Heaney-esque type reference, around the same time the man had penned his 'Digging' poem.

By the time the Land Commission was dissolved in 1992, both my mother (1968) and my father (1975) had long since departed this life.

And from the job I held then 'pushing a pen' in writing, I marvelled at my mother's foresight and couldn't help but wonder what would have happened to my brother or myself had the Commission come down in favour of our family when dividing up the land beside us.

THE GREAT LAND DIVIDE

Seven

The Visit

THE farm of the sixties was a little isolated republic of its own – often when you were out working in the fields, you saw or heard very little from one end of the day to the next.

With just my father and brother for company, it was often a very boring day as after the usual banter about horseflies around our faces or rain coming in from the west, we would get into a rhythm of work with the thoughts in our heads the only means of conversation open to us for hours on end.

It meant that any distraction was embraced like a sort of lottery win. A man walking his dogs on the road or chasing rabbits in another field became a momentary distraction. Sometimes a neighbouring land owner would drop in to see if we could lend him our mare for a few hours work.

Other times our cousins would descend on us unexpectedly to help us get over the line with the hay-saving, if as they also saw it, there was rain threatening to come in from the Galway direction.

Those were the occasions when you were relieved of being a pre-teenage adult worker and allowed to go explore across the woods or the bog. Roles were automatically redirected. My cousin and myself were sent to gather wood to make a fire so that we could drum-up – boil the kettle and prepare food which was always brought in a brown cardboard box.

Those days flew while others when we were on our own dragged out.

One year our Dublin cousins came down for a long weekend with my uncle. His boys were older and that instantly made them much more appealing to us.

They were curious about everything that they came across from horse and gig-rake to the nooks and crannies of our yard when they got home from the fields.

My uncle had the magnetism of a film star – he seemed to dwarf my father both physically and in his talk about times past and what he had got up to as a youngster.

My brother and I were enthralled by him and by extension, his sons who seemed to enjoy hiding behind the cocks of hay we were making. They also loved it when we introduced them to our own trees which we invited them to climb.

My brother had one special tree which he knew how to climb better than anyone else while mine, though not as tall, was a tricky challenge.

We were both severely crestfallen when we saw how easily they pulled themselves up through our branches to the very top. Their youngest boy gave the Tarzan roar when he ascended, a noise that echoed right across the valley.

My mother was still alive at the time and it was only when we had gone home and had our supper that our uncle and entourage reunited with us. He had brought them to meet a friend of his from his young days and then they had gone to my aunt's – where they were staying – for food.

And finally he had come home to the house he was reared in to talk into the night. My mother was a bit like myself and loved the distraction of company but as the night went on, you could see my father was getting increasingly irritated at the stories from the past my uncle was dragging up.

My mother had a unique way of catching his eye and delivering a silent message with her look – it said: "Go with the flow."

The three cousins were a bit restless too as the evening turned into night and my mother told my brother to bring them down the yard to play for a while.

Down in the far shed the eldest one of them found an old gun that my father used at harvest time to scare crows away from the barley.

Immediately I became frightened as the eldest cousin started pointing the gun in our direction and without touching the trigger, made gunshot sounds with his mouth. He then went back out into the yard, saw a black whitehead calf in his sights at the end of the hayshed and pulled the trigger.

A real shot rang out and the calf dropped as if he had been taken out by an expert marksman. My cousin looked disbelievingly at the gun as if to say – "how did that happen."

Within seconds my father and uncle were at our sides trying to make sense of the sound.

"What the hell is going on," my father asked with a voice barely disguising the true annoyance I knew he was feeling.

"It just went off," the oldest boy said in a pronounced Dublin accent. My uncle snatched the weapon out of his grasp and uncocked it in case it went off again.

Away from the post mortem which went on in the kitchen for half an hour after the incident, I kept thinking that it could have been me instead of the black whitehead calf that was dead if my cousin had decided to pull the trigger when he pointed the gun in my direction in the shed.

There was general relief when the visitors decided shortly afterwards to call it a night and go home to my aunt's house.

The following day as we worked down in the hayfield, their car drove in through the gateway and out onto the grass. This time there wasn't the same excitement on seeing them but it broke the monotony and allowed us an earlier break than usual from grass-cocking the hay in readiness for piking.

My uncle talked to my father about paying compensation for the dead calf but he wouldn't hear tell of it.

"These things happen," he reasoned, though I felt that it was my mother's words I was hearing, even though they came out of my father's mouth.

The boys said sorry to my father in a mannerly way before deciding they would go off 'exploring' down the fields. My uncle encouraged my brother and I to go along with them to have a bit of fun, saying he would give my father a dig out with the work.

I was wary of the offer, as I knew before the day was out, these lads would find some trouble – and my worry was that this time I might not survive to tell the tale.

We ended up roaming into a neighbouring bog area about half a mile away. There was gorse everywhere and that seemed to attract their interest. Then the oldest cousin asked me to open my hand.

Without understanding I did as he requested. He thrust a match into it and made me swear that I would never speak of what was about to happen.

I wanted to protest but my vocal faculties had closed down and before I could speak, he lit the match and the dead grass which the visitors had collected and put under the gorse bush was burning through the prickly undergrowth.

Within minutes the fire was eating into the gorse all around it with an ever elongating tongue of flame. I was sick in my gut. They whooped and hollered at the scene but like me, my brother had turned white as a ghost.

He warned the boys that we would have to call the fire brigade or the whole bog would end up in flames.

They seemed inclined not to believe us and began to try to dampen down the fire by beating at the blazing thicket with sticks which were littered on the ground of the wooded area.

My uncle appeared out of nowhere, having probably read the smoke signals from where he was working alongside my father. He neither appeared agitated nor amused at what he was witnessing but he directed us to go ahead of the fire.

He ran over a short time later to where there was a clearing behind him; then he lit another fire which he encouraged by pushing the bushes away from himself to eat back towards the other fire coming in his direction.

Within a few minutes, the two fires had contested with each other for the remaining unburnt gorse and a short time later, both fell as if they were opponents spent by the exertions of battle.

When we returned to our field, my uncle told the story of what had happened to my father, who said he was about to follow us when he noticed the smoke had disappeared from the sky.

He asked us what had happened and we stuck rigidly to the line that we had chanced upon the fire and had tried to put it out. The oldest cousin embellished the story by saying that he had seen two young guys scurrying away as we approached the area that was ablaze.

Although I had recently made my first confession and Holy Communion and knew how serious deliberate lies weighed on a Christian's soul, I had been sworn to secrecy and said nothing to add or detract from the story. I knew there would be a time later when I would have to come up with a way to present my sin of omission to the priest in confession.

My mother and aunt arrived down in the mid-afternoon with flasks of tea and sandwiches and biscuits. This had never occurred before because it was nearly a mile and a half journey and normally we made our own tea and brought the food with us.

They too heard about the burning gorse and whatever about my aunt believing our story, my mother immediately looked at my brother and then me to see our response to what she was being told by the oldest cousin.

My brother lowered his gaze away from hers and I did the same. We could possibly lie to others but there was no hiding place with our mother.

When we got home that evening – somewhat earlier

than usual as the work had been completed thanks to all the pairs of hands we had to help – it was the first, and only item on her agenda.

I deferred to my brother, who in fairness to him, stuck to the party line.

She dismissed him as if she didn't need any verbal evidence from us.

"Those lads did it but were you two involved?" she asked.

In unison both of us shook our heads while again averting our gaze from hers.

"That proves it, you were involved," she stated. "They lit a match and couldn't wait to see the bushes go up in flames."

The next day we headed down to turn the newly cut meadow in the Five Roods. It was the first time ever that I wished there were only the three of us – my father, my brother and myself.

If a calf had been shot on the first day and half the townsland set on fire the second, what lay in store today, I wondered worriedly inside my head?

To my surprise, they didn't appear at all. At first I was relieved but then curiosity set in and I wondered why they had failed to show.

Around lunchtime my aunt appeared on her bike but this time there was no food. She was my uncle and father's younger sister who was forever cast in the role of peacemaker in our family.

She seemed a little ruffled and when my father

asked her if she was alright, she nodded, adding: "I just needed to get out for a cycle to cool down after the morning I had at home."

Again the three boys were central to her story. While my aunt and her husband and my uncle were having breakfast, the three lads had gone into the sitting room where the budgie resided and decided to release it out of its cage. She told my father they had done so to see which of them would be the first to catch the bird and put it back.

"Unfortunately, I always open the top windows in the summer to let fresh air in and once the budgie flapped its wings outside the cage, it immediately escaped through the open window out into the garden," my aunt explained.

This time the boys owned up as to what had happened, thereby initiating an immediate hunt of the outside area. About an hour after the escape, the budgie was found dead with its plumage scattered around its final resting place. The neighbour's cat had spotted its unsteady flight path and had taken its chance when the opportunity arose.

My uncle's patience snapped when he saw what had happened and within five minutes he had loaded the three lads and their belongings into the car and headed back to Dublin.

"He was going to swing around in the car and tell you but I said I'd come down later and explain why they had gone back," she told us.

My father nodded instead of saying thanks, his gesture giving the message that he understood.

She then went across to where she had left her bike and walked it towards the gate.

"Isn't it very quiet down here?" she said, as if she had listened to the silence of the fields for the first time. "You'll miss the noise without them," she added with a chuckle as she walked along up onto the road.

My father sucked on his pipe and said nothing. My brother continued working on the swathe of hay he was turning without looking up.

Me? I felt happy that, horseflies aside, there would be nothing to interrupt our work for the rest of the day.

Eight

The Day Bobby Kennedy Saved My Bacon

YOUR last day at primary school is a sort of right of passage. You are moving onwards and upwards and are no longer one of life's 'small fry'. I'd seen lads in years above me hug and shake hands on the day of departure – even though many would go on to the same secondary schools. There was always a healthy minority who would never again sit down as classmates as they had done for the previous eight years.

The school was like an army barracks; every year you moved up a class and every year you got more stripes.

By sixth class you and your classmates were the biggest boys around – on the U-12 and U-14 football and hurling teams and a part of all special school occasions – in my brother's year it was for the golden jubilee of the 1916 Rising when everyone learned at least the first part of the Proclamation.

Our school was run by the Franciscan Brothers who were still very powerful in the community and considered for the most part firm but fair disciplinarians by tradition. The late sixties was still a time when there were people answering the call to vocations and my world changed when a young trainee brother came into our classroom.

He was studious looking and intense and totally devoid of humour but he had an insatiable appetite to turn pages and he expected us to keep up with him.

He also loved exams – it seemed that every other day he had us building up to an Irish grammar or an algebra or an English-Irish poetry test. By our reckoning if he had come any sooner than the middle of May for his six week 'hands on' training, we would have been matriculation material by our designated last day at school, June 28, 1968.

Of course it suited the principal, a big stout man with a temper that exploded like Vesuvius – which luckily was not too often – but had spectacular consequences when he did.

'Tubby,' as we called him, in introducing his trainee made it clear that we should all treat him with the utmost respect – warning that there would be dire consequences if he got reports of any misconduct.

Initially, we were so delighted not to have his threatening volcanic persona in our presence that we were well-behaved and of general benign disposition to the new boy-man.

The young monk appeared to grow in confidence with every passing class so that by the beginning of June, he was flexing his own muscles – clipping the odd ear and graduating to full wallops across the head if he perceived any stubbornness to his commands.

It got to the point where four or five of us began to yearn for 'Tubby' such was the constant fear of violence from this new source.

My friend, who also happened to be the best fighter in the school – which is why I made sure he was my friend – felt that we had to get respect back or we'd never make it to the end of the month.

He suggested throwing something at the young buck and then surrounding him if he tried the sort of violence that was becoming the norm.

I wasn't so sure about throwing a sliotar or an inkwell in his direction as I was mindful that 'Tubby' would take our heads off if he heard of such rebellion.

And so it came to pass that the best fighting boy took on the trainee monk on his own and laid down a marker of sorts.

When he failed to answer a question, the young master lashed out with a massive swing of his right hand but found a stiff arm knocking his intended stroke off target.

My friend then caught the monk by his robes and showing great strength for a 14-year-old, pushed him backwards like a scrum on the front foot against retreating opposition.

It was the boy's good luck that the Principal had driven off on an errand shortly before this incident took place and probably even more fortunate that he failed to return for the rest of the day. Otherwise, we would have felt the power of his retaliation.

By the following morning, however, the word had percolated to the staffroom that the oldest and biggest boy in sixth class had thrown the trainee teacher around like a rag doll.

By mid-morning, 'Tubby' interrupted our class without by or leave and caught our attention in no uncertain manner by thumbing down on the desk as he moved his replacement to one side at the top of the classroom.

He was livid and scanned our faces to find the culprit he wanted to make an example of.

Cowardice and fear are things most people detest but sometimes they can be used to help the brain undertake some very intellectual movements long before others think of them. And that was where I came in.

Aware that the Principal's absence on the day of the fight was pure serendipity, I knew there would be hell to pay the following day over what had happened.

Accordingly, I suggested to my friend that he should not only stay at home the next day but pretend that his neck or back was *in bits* so as to scare off any thoughts of reprisals when he returned.

"Where is he?" boomed the Principal's voice. "Where is he?"

The trainee shuffled towards the principal, and with his hand up to his mouth, advised his elder that the offending boy was "as láthair inniu".

That seemed to defuse the situation as both spoke, under their breaths, for about a minute. Indeed the Principal appeared to be about to depart when a little voice in my head told me that I had better act fast or it would merely be a case of violence postponed rather than erased permanently.

"Sir," I lied, "he had to go to the doctor after what he done to him."

For a second 'Tubby' had to squint to see where my voice was coming from. Then when he heard what I had said, he shouted: "It's *did* you imbecile, not done."

I wasn't too bothered at the put down over my grammar and instead looked to see if my statement had landed any sort of blow. I thought I detected a flicker across the face of the younger man but the Principal's face was impossible to read.

On the next day, my friend was back in school replete with neck brace. Class was on by the time I arrived and he winked as he saw me survey the prop he had requisitioned for the day.

When the head teacher came in to complete the discipline task he was forced to abort the previous day, the presence of the neck brace appeared – as I'd hoped – to scare him off his mission of revenge.

Once again both men headed into a corner where they undertook a conversation in lisped whispers. At the end of their chat, the Principal addressed us – again warning that if there were further *contretemps*, there would be trouble.

During all my years in school, the one thing that has got me in hot water more than anything was my inability to keep a laugh under wraps.

As the Principal was finishing off his little damnation warning to the class, the boy with the neckbrace turned around to me, giving me a thumbs up and a big wink as if to say – "well done, we beat them there."

My involuntary chuckle came from the manner of his wink – which was so exaggerated that I found it incredibly funny.

I knew straight away it was a mistake; the noise drew two pairs of daggers in my direction from the top of the class.

"You," said 'Tubby'. "You'd want to watch your Ps and Qs."

I wasn't so much worried by his warning as the look of intent that I could read in the young teacher's eyes. It said I was now public enemy Number 1.

At break-time I told my pal as much and he said he would look after me if the young monk tried anything.

I complimented him on his neckbrace, saying it had taken the wind out of the enemy's sails and he said he saw it lying around at home and after my suggestion about an injury, it was easy to do the rest.

My intuition about the trainee teacher was right; he had me up at the blackboard above and beyond the call of duty solving problems or finding the 'tuiseal ginideach' of some Irish sentence.

I knew it was only a question of time before I felt his knuckles bearing down on me.

On the Thursday he split us up according to what our parents' various professions were; in my group there were about eight farmers' sons with their hands up.

As it happened I was asked the last question; the others had answered easy enough queries such as what time of year lambs were normally born or when beet was harvested.

When it came to me he asked me to comment on the influence Jethro Tull had on agriculture. The only time I had heard that name was from an English boy who lived near Luton in England and who came home every year next door to us and raved about this rock band as the next big thing.

For the life of me I didn't know why the young teacher was asking me how a rock band could influence agriculture but it made me all the more determined to make him look silly.

"Well," I said. "I think when their music comes on the transistor the cows milk more."

In the same way as I had not heard of the man who revolutionised how grain seeds were sown three centuries before, he had never heard of Ian Anderson and his band and understandably thought I was taking the mickey.

Having been already earmarked as someone who needed manners put on him, I was now offering him *carte blanche* to attack me.

This he duly did. Although he was no body builder, he was probably in his early twenties, and as a young 12-year-old, I had no chance against him in the physical stakes. I retreated into a corner where he proceeded to take his frustrations out on me.

Two things brought about a premature end to the one-sided fracas.

The first occured when my friend, neckbrace clearly not holding him back, came to my aid when he caught the teacher from behind and spun him to the ground.

From then things seemed to proceed in slow motion; the classroom door opened just as my friend had stood back from the teacher to allow him to rise.

Instead of the expected anger, the Principal's face was contorted in sorrow and for a moment I thought he was going to cry. He regarded the pathetic appearance of the young teacher as he struggled to get his monastic habit and robes properly back on his body and then he looked at my friend and pointed to the corridor.

"Sir,' I shouted. 'It was me, not him."

Accepting my word without further questioning, he signalled me to follow him. I did, my knees knocking in anticipation of what I felt sure would be administered in the name of summary justice.

I brought my schoolbag out with me and left it outside the Principal's office as I entered; I had a premonition that there would be no going back.

By the time I got to his office, he was already seated behind his desk trying to tune the dial to BBC.

He looked at me, pointed at the chair and said: "Sit down while I see if I can get this thing to work properly."

The noise from the radio came and went in waves; he put it up to his ears, shutting virtually all of the sound off from me. I was perplexed at what was happening but began to sense that maybe this could be a day where I might escape the excesses of his wrath.

After what seemed an age, he put the transistor down on the desk in front of him and declared with a rare vulnerability: "Bobby Kennedy has just been shot in California."

This also triggered an immense sadness in me because since JFK had been gunned down in Dallas five years earlier, every Irish family, including ours, had an interest in the welfare of the Kennedys.

"Some fella shot him three times the radio is saying," he muttered abstractly as he looked out the window into the big yard.

I kept my head down, trying to sneak periodic looks at his face to read his mood.

He gave several loud sighs; each time I shuddered slightly. I thought they might be the forerunner to his thoughts returning as to why I was sitting opposite him in his office.

But they weren't. Then after a long pause, he gazed at me before asking: "What happened in there just now?"

I edited everything down for him to one sentence which I felt was totally true.

"I don't think the new teacher likes me," I said, sounding, I hoped, a little sad at such an outcome.

'Tubby' raised his eyebrows at the curt nature of my reply, and added: "I think you're right."

He told me to go home and come back on Monday.

As I got up to go, he engaged me in chatter again.

"He would have been president, you know," he said as if I was an equal.

I nodded in agreement.

"All's changed, changed utterly as Yeats said," he stated before waving me off out of his sight and into the freedom of the corridor.

In a way he was right. Bobby Kennedy was buried the following week and Richard M Nixon was released on the world as the next US President.

I had promised 'Tubby' that I would return for the Monday but I made my mind up that with only a few weeks to go, I would stay at home and get to work on the farm ahead of the season for a change.

Surprisingly my father didn't give out to me when

I told him that I had a row with a young monk and wasn't going back. I had expected him to tell me I would do no such thing but he just nodded his head as if talking internally to himself. I would later find out that he had a similar exit to his primary school days himself.

I never got to say goodbye to my classmates and never felt the sense of union that I had with the other 30 or so boys over the previous eight years.

And as for the young monk – that day was the last I ever saw or heard about him again. With my mother dying in late summer of that year, I went away to boarding school and lost contact with the order and the teachers, including the trainee.

However, the older I get, the more I regret the adverse indoctrination he got during his teacher training among us.

My hope is he learned enough from it either to make teaching his profession and the monastic life his mission or to switch into something that suited his talent and his temperament best.

Nine

A Dark Day In The Town

IT was a morning like any other in the town. As the church bells chimed, the workers heading for the factory left their bicycles against the railings, entered the porch hurriedly, knelt in the back pews, said a quick prayer and blessed themselves from the holy water font as they exited through the main doors.

It was a morning like any other in the town – except for one thing. The rumour had circulated for some time that there might be problems with the factory production of jute in an era that was rapidly expanding into plastic.

By the afternoon, the large workforce from the town and indeed surrounding towns and counties would know if their weekly wage packets every Friday would be a thing of the past.

The town held its breath; the pall of a death hung over its busy main street and square as if a doctor was attending a patient's bedside and was about to deliver a damning diagnosis.

In the shop opposite the church, the family who had recently purchased the going concern of grocery, bar and farm supplies was talking animatedly to the staff. They knew that fewer pay packets to spend in the town meant less money to go around.

The hardware shop across the road held an *ad hoc* meeting. There, the man who drove the van, the owner, his brother and my uncle looked out on the square after the morning mass and wondered would it ever be the same again.

Across the square the post mistress was unlocking the front door into the premises as the two postmen on duty mounted their bikes – each with a sack full of letters to be dispensed around the town.

The postman on the country run was bringing out a few parcels to put into the basket on the front of his bike – his cycle would necessitate climbing several hills before he would reach the valleys – where he would drop off letters and parcels at the appointed addresses.

Two brothers ran the busiest little pub and grocery in the town – one whistled as he slung open the timber-shuttered side-gate into their premises; the other pushed in bags of animals feedstuffs – pollard and clarinda – in a wheelbarrow.

The man in the slaughterhouse next door wished him a good morning as he nipped past, gesturing with a sharp flick of his right hand towards his mouth to the other brother to throw him up his morning starter. The shopkeeper obliged by giving the thumbs up without a word needing to be exchanged.

In the butcher's stall from where he came the owner was busy sawing loin chops from a lamb's carcass. The butcher's older brother had a brown shop-coat on and was weighing a half pound of lamb's liver for a woman with a large family. She had arrived early to get one of the cheapest meat parts of the lamb killed that week – she had many hungry mouths to feed and sustain.

She watched the man cut the liver expertly with his sharp knife as she talked absent-mindedly of the big decision that would be made that day; the man nodded in acquiescence, though he was too concentrated to hear what she was saying.

Only as he placed the offal in thick brown paper and skilfully applied a twine wrap with sudden hand movement as if he was a magician did he hear her say: "The word, I believe, isn't supposed to be good," but added: "Where there's life there's hope."

Twenty yards down the street, the big, gregarious man from the grocery shop and pub next door was standing out at the front of his premises, his hands positioned theatrically across his chest as he surveyed the comings and goings of the townspeople.

His eyes darted first one direction and then the other; up to the square before then sweeping down along the other side of his street where the two drapery shops nestled on either side of a pub. All three were still unopened at that time of the day.

As his eyes travelled down to the other end, there was plenty of activity in the corner shop with workers filling the supply truck with produce for delivery to the outlying farms. He waved warmly at one of the men, and he answered him back with a salute of his right hand to his temple as if he was an army foot soldier meeting an officer.

The two newsagents on either side of a tangential street to where the big man still stood had delivered the morning national papers around the town and would now await the arrival of the local newspaper before midday to see if they had been versed in what might happen at the factory.

The brothers in the bigger newspaper shop leant on either side of the big wooden counter discussing the fear of closure with the man they employed to tend their garden and do handiwork around the house.

"I can't see it happening. Sure it's been running well here since shortly after the famine," the workman said with a sense of bafflement over why such a sword of death should hang over a town's head.

The Parish Priest walked in, causing the brothers

to stand erect and welcome him. "I can't remember what I've come in for," he said, a look of embarrassment sweeping his face.

"Was it for a paper, Father?" said the older of the brothers.

"Aye, that's it, the Irish Press," he said, relieved that the problem had been sorted.

"We already delivered them up to the sacristy after eight o'clock Mass," one of them explained.

When the priest left the shop, he drove his Volkswagen around the back of the town and arrived up at the bank facing down into the square. He entered there just as the doors were being opened to the public and was greeted by a clerk who had recently arrived from down the country.

"Do you know what I'm here for?" he asked the young man, as courteously he held the door open to allow him to go in.

"No, what are you here for, Father?" said the bank official.

"That's alright," said a voice from behind the counter. "Father, come in to my office and we'll sort out that matter we discussed last week."

The priest looked blankly at the bank manager and tried to take in what he had said. The man gently took his arm and guided him across the main public banking area to a room that acted as his office at the side.

They would be two of only a handful of people in the

town, who when they met that day, would not discuss the worry hanging over the residents.

Up in the factory itself, the hum of machines had a mollifying effect on the staff as they tried to work normally though their morning shift though every time a manager either entered or exited from the main area, their attention followed to see if it was to make the announcement.

In a time when only the rich had a house phone and the term social media hadn't even been coined, the word still spread like wildfire.

When the man in the factory finally made the announcement, hundreds of people heard the bad news simultaneously.

The factory was losing money hand over fist and it would be scaling down dramatically with the loss of several hundred jobs.

Having heard the announcement, one man, rightly feeling no longer obliged to clock in and out, bolted for the town and had dropped the word in the shops where people congregated.

"The factory is closing," he said half out of breath with his run in from the car.

He stood as the town had seen him stand many times at the door of a house where a death had occurred, and speaking into the distance, remarked: "Our little town is banjaxed."

By the time he had done the main street, the word had shot to the four corners as in every shop there was an emissary ready to dart further afield and bring the dark news.

Every house had someone working there or had an indirect dependence of some sort on the place.

By the time the Angelus bell rang, signifying a call to prayer at six o'clock that evening, the town was in mourning.

Even as a younger person listening to the adults that night, the sense of fear was palpable. Older men spoke of never being able to find a job again because of their age profile while younger ones spoke of "heading over to England."

The pubs were full that night – the news had brought people out to talk together, to share the unknown they would now experience.

They were mourners at a wake but without a corpse.

The world had become a different place with the news of the closure.

In the weeks and months and indeed years afterwards, the town I grew up in and knew so well changed from being an integrated and confident community to one thrown to the mercy of a big world which had more than its own share of worries to preoccupy itself with.

Something died that day for the community and I'm not sure it was ever replaced.

Ten

The Turncoat

THERE we were waiting and waiting for the cavalcade to arrive. Some said it had only left the other town half an hour before... others claimed it would be here imminently.

My friend and I had walked all the way down to meet it at the town's entrance and became part of the celebrations from the old Court House just before it swung into River Street.

The politician – a gentle and truly popular man – and his entourage were approaching on the victory parade.

We could hear the music accompanying them and the energy of the sound beating out from the loudspeaker mounted on the lorry.

The townspeople had turned out in force to be part of the historic occasion and they were giddy now in anticipation as they lined either sides of the street all the way up to the square.

It was Saturday evening but even the small farmers from the outlying holdings had completed their chores and cleaned up early on this particular occasion. They too didn't want the night to pass without feeling fully part of the experience.

People had dressed up and there was a smell of cleanliness in the air; carbolic soap from the skin, brylcreem from the hair and the ladies with their different perfume aromas wafting across the early summer air.

Everyone was in good humour, the men smoking pipes and cigarettes were making jokes and laughing heartily at the wit that flowed effortlessly.

I waved to the man who had a farm on the other side of our largest and longest field. He spat in his hand, lifted his cap, rubbed the spittle across the top of his head in an attempt to make the black mane sit down better.

He didn't appear to recognise me away from the land and instead shouted over to another farmer on the opposite side of the road. "Up the Republic."

The man laughed at his shout, saluted him with a fist pump and shouted back in agreement: "Up the Republic."

As the lorry rounded by the Quaker House and inched its way over the river bridge, a roar went up as if a sound-blast had been detonated under the vehicle.

It seemed to rock and jolt the wheels before steadying itself and moving forward again.

The farmer who didn't recognise me took his cap off again and shouted.

"Here he comes...one of ours."

The cloth caps were thrown skywards as the throng exulted in unison to another of the man's promptings: "One of ours," they shouted loudly to let him know how they felt.

An Anglia car suddenly weaved past the lorry – much to the chagrin of those watching – and the man driving kept his eyes firmly fixed on the road. He was like a hare trying to escape the clutches of a greyhound and his eyes danced furtively as he looked for empty space on the street to get away from the flowing masses behind him.

The man across from me shouted – "Blueshirt" – and the crowd laughed loudly at his quip as if the utterer was a genuine comedian.

The man in the car didn't hear him but I knew that he was always working hard and was now only getting home from the bog. The town may have had celebration on its mind, but for him, he still had cows to milk.

My friend and I escaped the stewards who were trying to keep the people off the road. We made our way towards the centre of attraction and jumped onto the back of the open-top lorry after it had navigated the bridge. We hopped up and pirouetted in mid-air so that we landed triumphantly on our backsides at the tailboard end. We sat with the palms of our hands on either side of us as we dangled our legs over the back. It meant that we were now looking backwards at the crowd and seeing their reaction to the new Dáil deputy as he waved down at them as he passed by them.

Two other lads from our class tried to get up beside us but my friend told them we were on official work for the party. He winked at me and we both felt important; he had upgraded our status to be part of the official cortege.

Homemade tricolours fluttered from the houses on the main street as the women and small children stood at their doorways and saluted the slowly passing group.

They shouted up to the man and it sounded from the back of the trailer that the criss-crossing of shrieks would burst the tyres on the lorry and all our eardrums as well.

My friend muttered something to me but I couldn't hear what he said. We laughed and he gave me a 'thumbs up' sign to say it didn't matter. Things were good.

The Irish music acted as the background to the shouting, the cheering and the whistling from the swarms of mouths opening and closing in a swelling cacophony.

It was great fun. My friend's family were spread all around and so were many of the other school pals' families I knew.

They shouted slogans about de Valera and Republicans and Lynch and the party.

The atmosphere was like a *Mardi Gras* – the band struck up a popular tune and the smell of food invaded out nostrils from the chip shop across the street.

Night was closing in rapidly by the time the cavalcade stopped outside the politician's house and after several minutes standing still in homage, it jolted forward again. The square was lit up by special lights as the lorry – on which we had steadfastly clung onto despite efforts to swat us off by stewards – edged into its preserved parking place facing out into the square.

None of my family was there except for my uncle who was the master of ceremonies. He wasn't really an uncle but his brother had married my father's sister and from that we were encouraged to address him as "uncle" whenever we met him.

"A great night for Fianna Fáil," he declared to one and all.

The crowd gave a throaty roar into the night that rebounded from the buildings upwards and spilled out into the hills of Aughamore, Raheen and Kilbride on the outskirts.

"Up the Republic," my uncle went on, working the crowd into a crescendo.

My friend loved the commotion of the rhetoric and joined in by shouting back and lifting my arm and his in unison.

"Up the Republic," we too shouted from the lorry's edge which we had still managed to keep as our own area to view proceedings.

Then a heavy hand descended on my shoulder and spun me around facing into the crowd.

"You," said the man who had just manhandled me. "What are you doing here. Sure ye're all Blueshirts. Don't tell me you are a turncoat as well?"

That Blueshirt word again. And now another – turncoat. What were they going on about?

People around him and even some of the crowd nearby laughed lustily at his loud chastisement and without understanding what he was talking about, I felt myself blush deeply as a feeling of unworthiness to be there swept through me.

"Ah, will you leave the goson alone," said a kindly neighbour. Then by way of mitigation, he added: "Sure weren't his mother's side all Fianna Fáil?"

My friend looked at me and it seemed he too was wondering what was going on. He could see that I had become upset. Instinctively, we both jumped down from the lorry and onto the concrete path. He pointed to the front and said we should try to get up nearer the stand where the speeches would come from.

I told him to go ahead as I had to be home to deliver the milk to the neighbouring houses before they went to bed.

He protested that it would be no fun without me but by then, I had turned and burst through the crowd, fighting back tears at the memory of my public humiliation.

My uncle was still speaking in the background and even as I wriggled free of the crowd and began running homewards, I could hear his words. "A great night as one of our own comes back to the town as a Dáil deputy."

I raced away now from the madding crowd into the anonymity of the darkness. Thoughts flickered through my mind like ticker-tape statements... imposter uncovered at celebration...a Blueshirt spy in Republican movement...the youngest turncoat ever.

It was the first night in my life that I had felt a sort of imposter, an outsider in a community which I'd believed was homogenous simply because we were all from the same place.

Every Saturday morning my mother sent me down the town to buy meat from this man who was now a member of Dáil Éireann. I would have asked my mother to explain the conundrum but she had passed away the previous summer. I couldn't tell my father where I'd been as I had left the fields early on the pretext that I was going to confession.

As a recently arrived teenager, I understood that once you told one or other of your parents a story, you were better off to stick with it.

When I got into the house, he was sitting at the fire, drinking tea and watching the television chat show on RTÉ.

"That was a long confession," he said as I headed from the kitchen to the dairy to get the milk ready for delivering.

"You needn't worry about that, I delivered it when I saw no sign of you."

I nodded my head and sat down in silence.

He must have sensed my unhappiness as he asked me if I had been at the rally in the square.

"I was hanging around there but it is only starting now so I came home," I said truthfully.

"You were right," he said softly. "If they saw one of us there, they'd be calling us Blueshirts or turncoats."

He took a sip from his cup of tea and spat into the ashes beneath the fire.

"We wouldn't want to give them the satisfaction of doing that now, would we?" he asked without looking in my direction.

A FLY NEVER LIT

Eleven

The Summer Invasion

UNLIKE previous generations who only came back to rural Ireland once in a blue moon on fleeting visits, by the 1960s, Irish immigrants in England had a much greater degree of freedom to return with their new families as they had amassed more wealth across the water.

Those who had gone across to our neighbouring Island and married, more often than not to someone who was brought up close to where they lived before emigration, made it a lifetyle to return to Ireland for weeks on end during the summer.

The English invasion saw parents repatriate with their native land while their offspring – sporting mostly London, midland or Liverpool accents – got a sense of their Irishness in their grandparents or other relatives' homes.

Within a matter of days, those newly arrived boys and girls had totally integrated into our community. They became pals with their cousins' friends and in my case one of those friendships has persisted down the decades to the present day.

As pre-teenagers, the emphasis was on playing soccer as these English lads regaled us with having gone to watch QPR, Luton Town and Southampton take on Manchester United or Spurs when they visited those smaller clubs in First Division fixtures.

As they became more Irish than the Irish themselves during those holidays by picking mushrooms, milking cows or making hay, they hated returning to their homes as much as we were sad to see them go.

Being young of course has many great advantages – you'd lightly say that time would fly until the following summer and you'd actually believe it too.

Exposure to the diaspora on those holidays was more than just a diversion with new boys and girls in our midst; it was to get a taste of another world outside our own.

We were a tight-knit tribe, interacting with the same people in school, mass, football and hurling and even when swimming in the factory pond after long days on the farm.

The English born children spoke of different races, different cultures and Irish centres where they learnt about the land of their fathers and mother before they ever had set foot on Irish soil.

Like other ethnic groups, they were seen as Irish in their own British communities; the paradox was that they only ever felt English when they came among us.

Their parents were a study in themselves; always full of fun the first weeks home as they met up with old school friends, their moods became darker with the thoughts of returning as the days ticked down to departure.

At a time when national identity and sense of place was much keener than it is now, it was perhaps only natural that there would be sadness at the thought of leaving. Their lives were as exiles except for a number of weeks parole back in the bosom of where they grew up.

One of the most poignant moments I ever heard came from a man who sat down with my father on our front window sill the night before he was due to sail back to the UK.

As they smoked and gazed out on the world that passed by up and down the road, my father told him that he was a lucky man to have made such a go of life "beyant."

"A big car, the best of clothes and wads of cash, life doesn't get much better," said my father, throwing out the fishing hook in light-hearted banter.

What he got in reply was something that left him in no doubt about who had the real riches in life.

Taking a drag from his cigarette, the man then exhaled the grey smoke for what seemed like an eternity. He let the moment settle and then said: "Put a price on being able to look across the green field there every day, seeing the people you were born into and then going down the town where everyone knows who you are and what you are about.

"Oh I've heard them inside – the family – give out about people gossiping, but it's a helluva lot better than standing on a platform in some English railway station and wondering are you invisible. John Lennon was right ... 'all the lonely people.' I don't think there is one of us over there who grew up in Ireland who doesn't feel it in the heart every day of the week."

He lit up another smoke and looked at my father, who by this stage had left the sill and had hunkered down with his back against the front wall of the house.

"I often think that those of us who had to go abroad to earn a crust got a life, but a life less fulfilled than you fellas who are lucky enough to stay at home.

"I'm here now for a number of weeks and the amount of people who haven't a good word to say about the town astounds me. If they were over in some housing estate in one of the big cities, they'd appreciate the worth of going to watch the club play in the senior championship or following the county in Croke Park. That's me and that's my culture but now I have to listen to the BBC and follow the soccer teams because my young lad is into it.

"It's not the culture I'd have wanted for him. I'd love to see him playing Gaelic in the club's colours here. The sense of loss in not being able to pass down the Irishness I knew. It is the saddest gnaw in any exile's gut."

He stood up swiftly, threw the half consumed cigarette on the footpath and stomped on it.

"By the time the sun comes up in the morning, I'll be on the ferry from Dun Laoghaire and you'll be thinking of getting up to work on the farm. Cherish the gift that fortune has given you. I didn't when I lived here the same as everyone else, but I'd give a king's ransom to know that I could live out my days in around this little town."

My father was always a very sensitive soul and having got a lot more than he bargained for with his glib remark about a big car and wads of money, he rowed back considerably.

"You know, you are right. We never know what we have until it's taken away. Having said that though, you're a lucky man to have got such a lovely family and coming home ever year is a great half-way house between where you are and where you'd like to be."

His son and I were kicking a ball close to where the conversation was taking place and heard every word.

My new friend came over to me after a while and said: "Don't mind the old man, he won't be back in England five minutes than he'll be the life and soul of the party with all my friends and their dads."

"You heard what he did last year at the Grand National. He went up to Liverpool to meet up with all the Irish lads who were over and ended up walking in with the winner talking to the Queen herself.

"The Special Branch geezers nearly had heart attacks when they heard this man with an Irish accent right beside her. She obviously knew he was just being friendly and gestured to them to back off.

'Those pictures don't do you justice, Ma'am,' he exclaimed with a hint of roguery.

'Thank you so much,' she replied with a smile, before adding. 'Tell me, are you having a good day?'

'No, lousy! That's why I said I'd ask you if you had any tips for the next race?'

She chuckled at his boldness and his sense of humour.

'None,' she answered, 'but I hope you pick the winner.'"

My friend went on: "He ended up nearly getting an invitation to Buckingham Palace. And then he tells you that he's lonely and doesn't fit in over there."

As he spoke, his son glanced across to where the two grown ups were sitting and caught the look on his own father's face as he ended the conversation. I did too and saw something profoundly melancholic in his gaze.

I fancied the son saw it too. "He'll be fine once we get off the boat in Holyhead," he emphasised again.

"Every time before we go back, he gets a bit like this,

contrary and low in spirit; he then kicks out of it and by the time we're half an hour on the road back towards London, he starts counting down the days to next year's visit".

Twelve

The Bet

DURING my father's lifetime we never owned a tractor and only ever hired machinery in to cut the meadow or to do the harvesting.

Everything else was old-fashioned and traditional. We milked cows by hand, cut thistles with bill hooks and scythes, pulled ragworts or buachaláns as we called them with our bare hands and made hay with forks.

It sounds somewhat Amish-like but it was our little world up to the mid-seventies.

Mind you, it wasn't as if the lack of modernity had escaped our notice but our father's heyday was also the horse's and he wasn't for changing.

Neighbours and cousins had begun to embrace the new ways up to a decade earlier but we carried on the same old fashion; the same pony and cart as our means of transport to and from the land and the same mare to do the heavy work such as ploughing and hay making.

There was a belief in the heads of people from that earlier generation which went something like: 'If it costs money, it is not worth having.'

Tractors were a cost; fuel, repairs and constant services in garages. The mare ate grass from the fields we owned, drank water from the river and was therefore a much better proposition in my father's eyes.

His simple philosophy could be boiled down to saying that if change was to be brought in, it would have to pay for itself.

I had learned how to drive a tractor on my aunt's farm and told him they were able to do much more work in a day because of it and were therefore more productive.

He laughed me out of it; the reason they did more was there were seven of them and three of us – and he hinted that neither my brother nor myself, but me in particular, didn't exactly stand out when it came to quantity or quality of workmanship.

That was our way of going on. Invariably those bouts of philosophical discussion took place when we were sitting in the shade of the ash tree in the Square Field as we drank our smoky tea and ate the makeshift sandwiches one or other of us had thrown together from packages we bought in the shop on the way down from the homestead.

Such conversations had a habit of turning out in his favour. The weekend after we had spoken about the benefits of having a tractor, my uncle called in on his way home for the town.

He spoke a language full of problems with hydraulic lifts and reborings, giving the clear impression that a big job was required on his grey Ferguson.

My father could hardly contain himself as my uncle spoke of what his usual garage man had told him the cost would amount to.

No sooner had he bade his farewells than our senior man declared: "I told you a tractor was a robber on a farm. What he has to hand out now is the same as selling a bullock. Sure no farm around here could stand that."

For a man totally practical with money, it came as a surprise for him to say that when my brother was old enough he would consider buying a small car. I don't think logic came into this equation; it was more a case of being able to visit his younger brother whom he adored in Kildare and go those extra distances which up to then required the hiring of a hackney driver.

The last time we had done that, the driver insisted he was in a hurry to get back for a bingo run in the town, meaning that we had no sooner arrived in Monasterevin than he was jangling his keys for us to depart.

My brother and I were delighted at the prospect of a car and like the good liars we were when it suited, we swore a hole in a bucket that we would never ask my father to use it at night to go to dances or such occasions he regarded as a total waste of time.

It was decided that we would buy it the following summer and a salesman from the next big town was asked to come to our house.

He was a master of his craft; the first night he called he extolled the virtue of having a car to get to cattle marts and pick things up in co-ops, adding that we should go for a vehicle where the back seats could be put down. He then asked us what our preferred model was.

I was the only one to pipe up: "Anything but a Morris Minor."

He promised to return the following evening and my father brought in a neighbour who knew about cars to oversee the transaction.

It was this man's view that the Austin 1100 he brought as a first attempt for a sale was not suitable. After he had taken it for a drive, he left the engine running, told me to rev the accelerator while he went around the back to the exhaust.

As I revved it up and down, he smelt the fumes, shook his head and pronounced: "She's burning oil by the gallon."

Inside the house, the salesman seemed unperturbed with this expert's opinion. Instead he replied totally deadpan as he downed his whiskey and prepared to drive off: "Aye, most engines are inclined to burn oil alright."

He promised to call back the following Saturday evening after work with another car more suitable to our needs.

When he did, I was delighted with the look of the Austin Cambridge and frankly didn't give two hoots if this one burnt coal, oil or whatever. It looked the part and I could see myself driving off to a dance – despite earlier pledges to the contrary – and feeling a million dollars.

Such notions were soon dispelled when he explained that she was a 1966 model and was worth £750. I could see my father lining up a half a dozen bullocks in his mind's eye and saying he would have to give them away for the pleasure of a petrol guzzling piece of tin that would add costs at every turn.

"You won't get much for anything less," the salesman said matter-of-factly, though I could see he was beginning to flag as what he had hoped would be a quick sale was turning into something of a marathon.

Slightly crestfallen, he said he would be back one evening the following week. I knew in my bones that when he pulled up it would be in a Morris Minor. If so, I had decided to tell him to forget about it as we would go to some other dealer.

And so it came to pass. Without hearing him arrive outside, he had turned the latch and was in the kitchen before we were aware of his presence.

"I have the very car for you and at a good price, though the young lad here mightn't like it," he said, pointing in my direction. We all followed him outside to see a shiny black Morris Minor – ELI 711.

"She's a '64 model," he informed us, something that pleased my father as immediately he would have deduced that if a big Cambridge was £750, an older and smaller car might be half the price.

I was now the crestfallen one – how could I ever make an impression driving a car that was a glorified motorbike?

In spite of or maybe because of my indifference, there was a genuine feeling on both the salesman's side and my father's that they could do business. They went the full five sets before my father delivered his final volley of £425 as the end of his bargaining.

Being underage and my father being of a different disposition than learning how to steer a mechanically propelled vehicle, my brother was the one who became the official driver. He loved the car and so did the pony as it meant that for the first time in her 18 years, she could take days off as we drove up and down to the land to herd or work without her.

At first we were terrified of getting a spot of dirt on the pristine black outside of the car but as the weeks and months went by, we not only were driving it on the roads but in the fields as well.

Our legs almost became powerless as 'Herbie', which we (unoriginally) christened it, was used to drive for the mile and a quarter behind cows on the way home in the evening and later on the milk round to neighbours at night, the furthest of which were about 300 yards away.

As my father said in his laconic way: "I suppose I should be thankful that you're not using it to drive yourselves upstairs to bed."

The car changed the pattern of a lifetime that summer, much to my delight. Instead of having to pack up tea, milk, sugar, bread, butter, jam, tomatoes and ham for our food during the day as well as cups, saucers, spoons and knives, we simply jumped into the car and drove home in five minutes.

There we could do up a quick fry and have better tasting food to sustain us for the long afternoon, which in my father's estimation would go on until eight o'clock. Then he would tell one of us, but usually me, to go for the cows while the work was finished up by them.

Part of the hay saving was drawing the cocks home into the hayshed but also by making ricks in the corner of certain fields which stayed active during the winter months.

There was always a sense of accomplishment as we approached the final furlong in the summer-long activity from mowing meadows to actually securing the hay for fodder.

The first summer we had 'Herbie' on duty led to many great arguments about how much time we saved having the car to get us up and down to the land as against the travel by pony and cart. It probably saved us an hour and a half a day but my father pointed out that there was a cost from the minute you turned the key in the ignition.

With the final rick of the year close to completion, my brother came up with a great challenge to compare the traditional with the new. There were two cocks of hay left out in the field about a hundred yards from the corner where I was on top of the rick taking in the hay that the two others piked up to me.

Normally either my father or brother would drive the mare out to a cock, raise the hay about the butt with a fork or with their hands and put a thick rope around it. The mare would then slowly pull so that the rope gathered around the butt and forced the cock to glide across the aftergrass in towards the rick where it would be thrown up to me.

"I tell you what," he said challenging my father. "You bring the near cock in with the mare and myself and 'Herbie' will bring in the other one.

My father laughed at the challenge. "That thing wouldn't pull the socks off a dead man, never mind bring in a cock of hay," he said, with a tone as assured as if he was saying that water flows downstream.

"Will you bet 10p with us," I said down to him, siding with my brother for the fun of it.

"I'll give you ten to one," he said, smiling as he untied the mare from where she was grazing around the headland.

Immediately I jumped down from the rick, half-tripping in my eagerness to become part of the great race.

We didn't have another rope of similar length or strength to the one used behind the mare but we found a smaller one, which we doubled to make strong enough for the job.

My brother and I motored out across the field and he expertly reversed the car sufficiently close to the cock. Then he fixed the doubled up rope onto the toe-bar and told me to get behind. "Make sure you get the rope right under the butt or it won't be able to pull it," he advised me.

Across the field, my father had not only nonchalantly thrown the rope behind the cock but had jumped onto the back of it instead of taking the time to lift up the butt – a short cut that could have repercussions.

"Quick," I shouted to my partner in betting. "He's going all out for a quick take-off."

My brother revved up the venerable Morris Minor and slowly the slack ropes became more and more taut. The moment of truth arrived as the back wheels of the car began to bite into the grass for grip as it encountered the weight of the cock against it.

Slowly it inched forward and I used a fork behind the cock to help with this groundbreaking moment for mankind. For a moment, the engine struggled, shaking the exhaust and the fear crossed my mind that it would conk out.

I moved around to the front and used the fork to lift the butt of the cock upwards; immediately bringing a positive response from the car. By now it had picked up pace and as it did so it was obvious that it would not just pull the cock across the sea of green grass but could sashay as it went along.

And so it came to pass that at the very time man was walking on the moon, we made the earth-shattering discovery that a Morris Minor could pull a cock of hay on a small farm in the midlands of Ireland.

We looked across to witness my father go head over heels as the rope jumped up halfway on the cock forcing the top part, man and all, to become dislodged while a massive butt remained undisturbed behind them.

Despite the fact that it would mean extra work for us all later in the day, the sight of the old ways coming apart in the hands of my father was something so funny that it had my brother and I laughing at its memory for a long time afterwards.

We had won bragging rights for the day and that night – and he'd have to pay over £1 to us after losing his bet.

THE BET

Thirteen

Pulling Buchaláns

SUMMERS in Ireland are often anything but; with rainy days and even weeks punctuating the odd few days where there were bursts of sun and bright weather.

The months of June, July and August were the prime hay-making, turnip thinning, barley or oats saving times. Most of those crops, if not all, were highly dependant on good weather to harvest them properly ahead of the winter that would surely follow.

Every now and again a prolonged period of precipitation meant that, like it or not, we had to go out and work in the driving rain.

One such occasion happened on a year when the

crop of ragworts or buachaláns across the country was at a particularly dense level.

It led to an approach to me by one of the Gardaí s to say that our field in the hollow, known by us as The Church Field – as it was located behind the Protestant Church – needed to be tended to as it was in breach of the 1936 Noxious Weeds Act.

For sure there was a yellow sea of buachaláns there and as it was the nearest field to the town, the Gardaí needed to be seen to flex their muscles to get something done about it.

What they said was that unless we did the job very quickly, the weeds would spread and the following years 'crop' would be even tougher to eradicate.

"Sure if the three of ye get at it, you'd have it done in no time," the garda said to me with a smirk on his face.

When I went home, I apprised my father of the conversation with the long arm of the law. Initially he was embarrassed that he had to be told how to manage his fields by the police of all people.

During dinner as we looked out at the stair-rods of rain falling in the middle of July, he lamented the fact that because the field was so close to the town, he would never bring the sheep in for fear of being attacked by the dogs around the place.

He was proud of the fact that a mile down the road where we had most of our land, there was scarcely ever a buachalán's yellow head in any of the fields.

Sheep, he claimed, kept land clean by eating without

harm to themselves a lot of noxious weeds, and in particular the ragwort. But they couldn't solve our problem in the Church Field and to make matters worse, our plan to mow them down with the scythe and bill-hooks was ruled out by my father.

"You don't cut Buachaláns, you have to pull them," he explained, stressing that if we cut them and left them lying on the ground, they were poisonous and would kill the cows and cattle.

Our task then was to attack the three acres. By the time we had finished dinner – always eaten in the middle of the day – it was decided that we would "make a start" on the job that afternoon, even though the rain showed no sign of letting up.

Within five minutes of attacking the weeds around the gate, my father, brother and myself were soaked through.

The beads of wet blisters on the plants made the task even more difficult – our hands found it hard to grip as they slipped upwards on the moist stems – making it harder to pull them up, roots and all.

It was slow and tedious work, made all the more back-breaking because of the number of times we needed to re-grip the stems to get them to yield.

We worked for about two and a half hours, our coats saturated and our hats leaking the wet into our hair and faces. We had started the job from the near gate and had probably made 30-yards progress during that time, meaning it would take us about four days in total to get to the far ditch and end the onerous task.

The worst thing about the whole exercise was the smell of the noxious things and the way the yellow stained our hands. Back at the house, no matter how long we washed with soap and hot water, there were massive yellow stains similar to cigarette colouring on a smoker's fingers.

By the time we had pulled the last pocket of the ragwort in the elbow of the field, there was a series of substantial heaps of the weeds across the field.

It was evening time and my father copped one of the heifers – which had proven in calf later in the season than normal – eating at the petal on a stalk at one of the first bunches we had raked together.

He raced across the field shouting in his attempt to prevent the heifer from swallowing the weed. By the time he got there she had three quarters of it down her throat.

Around stock, he had a mesmeric way of working; the beast wasn't used to handling like the cows but he talked to her in such a way that she allowed him to approach her; then he caught the stalk of the buachalán and managed to pull even the half-chewed part of it out of her gullet.

Immediately he ordered that all the cattle be moved from the field because there was no way we would be able to take all the weeds away that evening.

We kept an eye on the heifer for the rest of the day

but by the following morning it was clear that she wasn't herself.

"She has poison in her system," said my father. "What we'll have to hope for is that it isn't enough to kill her."

We had tied her up in the cowshed and brought buckets of water to her in the hope that it would flush the contaminant out of her system.

By evening time the following day, she had gone down and was not inclined to get up. Worse than that, she had lost interest in eating or even drinking.

'I think we'll lose her," my father predicted. "Once they go down no matter what's wrong with them, they're never likely to get up again although it happened once with us when ye were young."

The garda who approached me to do the work in the first place came over the following morning to thank my father for the prompt way we had dealt with his request.

"The dearest bit of work I ever did to comply with the state," my father said to him as he beckoned to him to follow him down to the cow house.

As the garda arrived at the door of the shed, his eyes focused before he saw the body of the heifer, lifeless in the corner.

He looked at my father and myself, his brow furrowed as he tried to link the dead beast with our compliance with the Noxious Weeds Act (1936).

"She ate one we pulled," explained my father, "and there's one thing for sure – she won't eat another one."

Fourteen

The Fight

THE small man shuffled up alongside my brother and I outside the chapel. The wind blew at the lapels of his coat and tugged at his tweed cap which balanced precariously on the top of his head.

We had just put my father's coffin into the hearse and were waiting for the cortege to take off. Tradition in the town was to walk to the Parochial Hall and then have a car to drive the rest of the distance to the Monastery Cemetery about a mile out of the town.

From the time his funeral mass had ended, hundreds of locals had made their way up the church to where we sat in the front pew to shake our hands and pass on their sincere condolences.

Grief tears the heart out of you but those hands of friendship ushered in your direction help you to fight back. The visible form of support for the two of us was more than we realised at the time.

My brother not yet 22 and I had just turned 19; we were the newest 'orphans' in town.

Every hand was a lift back up for us in life; every awkward and whispered word of sorrow was a call of encouragement; every stolen glance a light shining hope back into our eyes.

Against that backdrop, the small man approached us outside at the chapel gates. He whipped his cap off with his left hand and then proffered his right hand first to my brother and then to me.

"What can I say?" he said as he looked beyond our shoulders as if he was trying to make out a figure in the distance.

"The best neighbour...," he added as he lifted his hand with the cap in it to dry his eyes.

Just then his son arrived outside of the railings with his car to ferry him to the cemetery.

The man's eyes had welled up again and he didn't see his son. When I told him he was there, he walked towards it and gave a slightly awkward, yet endearing wave back.

At the graveside a large crowd gathered in a knot around the old elm tree under which my father's grave had been dug. The priest proceeded with the burial service from under its canopy as the April shower spit angrily across the graveyard.

People tightened together to stay inside the embrace

of the elm branches that offered them protection from the elements.

From the other side of the grave I looked back out as the faces muttered their responses during the decades of the rosary.

The little man was beyond them out to my right side, his cap tightened in his two hands, his head slightly lowered as he deliberately clipped his responses.

Watching the earnestness of the little man, I wondered what my father must have thought as he looked down on this congregation sending him their parting good wishes.

As the priest shook holy water on his coffin and began his habitual prayer of: "Dust thou art and unto dust shalt thou return," a man with a hat pushed his way through the crowd and although slightly unsteady on his feet, maintained his forward thrust in the direction of my brother.

He slurred his words as he grabbed my brother's two hands in his own.

"How's your father?" he said quite loudly, immediately drawing the attention of the departing mourners with his indiscretion.

My brother smiled and using the black humour of the situation said: "I suppose he was often better."

"I'm down for a funeral," the man explained with a loud whisper as he leaned into my brother's ear. Standing near both, I immediately detected an overpowering smell of drink off the interloper.

'Is that right?" my brother said with a tone of agreement in the hope of parrying away any further chat from the stranger.

The inebriated man was oblivious to my brother's intention as he continued unabashed. "I haven't seen your father for a long while," he said as a perplexed expression crossed his countenance.

"Neither have I," quipped my brother back to him without ever trying to correct the man's faux pas.

I placed my two hands over my face to mute the spontaneous laughter that surfaced from inside at my brother's deadpan expression in such a situation.

The drunk man was an in-law married to my father's cousin in Dublin and had used the excuse of a funeral for a country expedition on the train. Apparently he had travelled down the previous night, not far but obviously too well, and had then completed his journey on the morning, too late for the mass but in time for the cemetery burial.

By then he had clearly forgotten which in-law of his had passed on, which resulted in his conversation about the deceased, my father, as if he was still alive.

We, both my brother and I, found the episode hilarious and it was that farcical cameo which in truth sustained us in the dark hours and days after the most important person in our lives had suddenly left us. We returned to it time and again, sometimes laughing and now and again becoming tearful as we said to each other: "I haven't seen your father for a long while."

The little man who was my father's friend was, however, incandescent at the behaviour and shook our hands again as we left the cemetery as if by way of apology for what he had just witnessed at our father's funeral.

We passed it off and told him that it wasn't worth worrying about.

It was a number of years later when the small man died that the memory of his friendship with our father surfaced again. No one knew why it was so deep and profound, especially as it was a friendship conducted from afar rather than in each other's company on a daily basis.

Returning from the same cemetery having laid him to rest, the grieving widow of the little man was an unexpected source, at a difficult time for her, of the mystery that had often surfaced in my mind.

"It was only lately that my man opened up to me about the reason for their closeness," she began, a white handkerchief in her hand and her handbag held loosely in the other.

"I would often say to him down the years when he would mention something about your father that for someone he admired so much, they seldom if ever got together.

"He would say that friendship was knowing that you had someone on your side if you needed him," she said, the memory of his reprimand causing her to chuckle rather than to feel sadness.

She went on: "Seemingly, like many great and distinguished friendships, theirs began in enmity. As boys, they were both small and stubborn and one day on the way home from school they began a fight which went all the way up the main street and some way back again.

"Both of them gave their all to best the other and it was only when a shopkeeper held on to your father and sternly told my man to go home that the fight was abandoned.

"That was a time when fighting and violence was widespread and good fighters had a respect among the other boys.

"However, the fights then weren't just among boys, the monks in the school were also well able to dish out beatings to young lads on a daily basis either with their canes or their fists.

"The monk your father and my husband had over their class was a particularly cross teacher who they knew was a deeply unhappy man because of his struggles with drink. Sometimes it was said that he was unable to stop himself once the red mist of violence descended before his eyes.

"Your dad was often his target as he was absent a lot from school from the time his own father, your grandfather, was poorly from the fall off a horse. But your dad only got stronger the more the monk beat him and according to my man, the monk would be drenched in sweat trying to get your father to say or do something but he wouldn't budge an inch.

"Although he was never big, he was broad-shouldered and by doing a man's work on the farm since he was nine or ten, he was as tough as old boot leather.

"My man saw it all up close because the two sat together in the classroom when they were in school. The seating arrangement among the class was selected by each teacher and it meant that even though the two boys had fallen out over their fight, they still had to sit side by side during their time in class," she explained as she paused for breath.

As we arrived where her son was already waiting for her, she leaned her frame against the car's closed back door to rest after the exertions of the half-mile walk down the road from the cemetery.

"Well," she continued, "my husband, God be good to him, told me what had happened after their row. The lads were in their final year and within a month, they would be leaving the school to go working full-time either in factories, firms or farms."

She blessed herself at their memory, fidgeted with her handkerchief and rubbed it gently under her eyes more as a habit than as a requirement to wipe away tears.

"The mad monk for some reason left your father alone on this day as he went about venting his anger on some new heads. My man distinctly remembered seeing blood spurt from the temple of the boy in front of him after the monk pounded his head against the inkwell on the desk several times.

"As bad luck would have it, my husband said he was so terrified at what he witnessed that instead of keeping his head down and maintaining a silence so as not to attract attention, he released a nervous intake of breath which sounded distinctly like a laugh.

"He said the harder he tried to stop himself, the more the unfortunate noise vibrated in his chest. The monk stopped in mid-violence on the boy in front to focus on what he saw as a clear case of insubordination by the smallest boy in the class.

"The chilling moments of realisation that he would face a savage beating by the monk caused my man to hyperventilate at the prospect of what lay ahead.

"As he struggled for breath, the monk threw a full-blooded right-hander at his face. Everyone in the class watched in trepidation, knowing that the power of such a blow on a small boy would have serious repercussions. It was then that your father deflected the punch from my man's head, taking most of the force of it on his own jaw.

"Your father took the blow, jumped up and pulled my man with him and before the mad monk could re-act, they were gone out the door and out of the school.

"Whether that surprised him or not, I don't know but the monk just sat there listless as the pair of boys scurried out of the class.

"Neither of them every went back to school. Instead they met every day for the few weeks that was left before they were due to end there anyway and spent hours fishing the river or walking the railway. Neither told their mothers and because the monk didn't inform his superiors as to what had happened beause of the embarrassment, no one in the school was any the wiser.

"I do know though that the monk left or was encouraged to leave some time later and was never seen again around these parts following the row. Maybe that day brought him to his senses or maybe he ended up in the gutter.

"I suppose," she said as she opened the door to sit into the car, "when you go through a terrifying situation like that together, there is a bond there that is never broken."

Her son turned the key in the car to start the engine and she shook my hand and said it was great of me to come down for the funeral.

"His is the condolence I remember most from my father's funeral," I told her truthfully. "The sincerity shone through so much that I would have travelled half way around the world to be here to honour him."

As her son looked slightly impatiently in my direction, I was about to turn away when she caught my hand again.

"Aye," she remembered. "That day stuck with him not only because it was your father's burial but because of the drunk that came out of nowhere to talk to the pair of ye.

"Do you know what I am going to tell you? Rightly

or wrongly, my man was convinced that because of the drink connection, that drunk had something to do with the alcoholic monk from their youth.

"He would speak about it a lot but I think in his own mind he thought it had something to do with the teacher coming back looking for forgiveness on your dad's grave."

Her son put the car in gear and she waved good-bye. "Ah, isn't it as good a way to think about it as any...that's what I always said to him anyway," she smiled as the car moved away.

THE FIGHT

Fifteen

The Glebe Legacy

IN life, in death, in sickness and in health, there was nothing as constant as land to the people of Ireland of the last century.

My grandfather on my mother's side had more sickness than health and by dying at 45 saw a lot less of life than he should have done.

Considered by my father to be the soundest man he had ever met – and that was long, long before he wed his eldest daughter in an arranged marriage – my grandfather was forever fighting just to survive.

When his own siblings finally got him sober enough to present him to my unsuspecting grandmother after he had come out of a deep drinking depression, there was an arrangement that as well as marrying into a fine upland farm, he would bring nine acres called 'The Glebe' as his dowry. This represented a reversal of the usual marriage rules where it was the wife-to-be that brought the smaller parcel of land or money into the marriage.

Like all pieces of land called 'The Glebe', this was once part of a clergyman's benefice but somehow over the generations had integrated into my grandfather's family holding.

He was now bringing it with him into marriage; it wasn't a fair exchange but it was better for two women, my grandmother and her sister, that they had a man about the place even if he had come at a cut-price.

Despite the fact that he would lapse back into his drinking ways within six months of marriage and continue to do so right through the rest of his life – although he manfully tried to abstain – he was beloved by his wife and three daughters and his sister-in-law.

They saw him for what he was; a flawed man but one who tried to be decent and honourable when not caught in the talons of demons he could not control.

It was a life of lows punctuated with the odd high and one of his happiest times was to see how his nine acres, 'The Glebe', helped the 'mother farm' become a stand-alone entity.

The field was a few miles away from where he lived and it felt like an expedition every time he had to make the journey there. But it was his pride and joy and he worked hard to keep it free of rushes by digging a drain in the lower part to ensure that the water didn't gather at the more inclement times of the year.

The field was his and he often brought my mother, his eldest daughter, on the bar of his bike when he rode down to check on the stock or the progress of the meadow he had growing there.

Several times he was approached by his own family to rent the plot back to them but he refused. This was because he had an amazing pride in watching over a possession which had gone back in time with his own family.

As time went by he confided more in his second daughter, my aunt, about how much it meant to him to go up and down to those few acres than the more fertile upland that he had farmed since he got married. While not a man to hold grudges, he felt that his own family had been relieved to cast him aside. This had hurt him, particularly the failure of his brothers to keep in regular contact.

He was cast out as a black sheep; a man with a drink problem who had been kept away from imbibing opportunities until such a time as a marriage to my grandmother could be brokered.

She was the big loser, if that is the right term, by being an innocent and unsuspecting partner to a man who would follow the smell of a whiskey cork to the butt of the wind.

As a very straight-laced woman, her discovery of his weakness when he went to the first fair day after their marriage must have shaken the foundations of her faith in man. Two weeks after it had taken place he appeared at the front door demanding she go to the town and bring back liquor to sate the unquenchable thirst he felt.

Whether love had entered their marriage by that stage – some six months after their wedding is a moot point, but it is fair to think that she must have believed herself married to a monster as day upon day, she ferried in the dark of night bottles of stout and naggins of whiskey to his bedside before finally succeeding in weaning him back to sobriety.

Judging from the memories of their daughters, there was tension in the house but as the children – three girls – got older, they also had an influence on his attempts to curtail his drinking.

My aunt's memory was that he would almost tie himself up rather than follow the craving when it hit him in his darkest moments. Once she claimed when he had surprised all of them by appearing in his good clothes during the day, a sign that he was heading to the nearest pub in the town, she jumped up unprompted as an eight year old and told everyone in the kitchen that she was going with him.

As he tried to escape out the yard onto the road, she ran after him, catching his leg and telling him that she would never let him go alone to meet his demons again.

She remembered looking up into his eyes and seeing his glisten with tears as he stood in the middle of the road, his body trembling in anticipation of alcohol. That was the day that the love of a child and her determination to save her daddy also shook his senses.

He lifted her up in his arms, kissed her, returned to the house and cried in front of the other women in his life – his wife, his sister-in-law, my mother and my two aunts.

From my mother's and my older aunt's account, that was the day that they became a true family and my grandfather gained the respect of his wife for putting them all ahead of the disease that would ultimately and prematurely kill him.

That came at a time when he had been on his best behaviour for a few years. However, his binging from his youth had obviously had its affect and he descended to death's door almost too quickly for the family to take in.

One day he was out in the Pump Field working; the next he was on the broad of his back in the bedroom, eyes closed and counting down to his last breath.

My aunt was returning from herding down in the field and was cycling on the bike past the same Pump Field when her heart rose. Over at the far headland, she saw her father walking towards the railway that ran behind their house. With a smile on her face she pedalled furiously towards their own front gate to be home before he arrived across the Bull Park field and in to the house from the rear.

My mother's sad face opened the door to her as she placed the bike against the window sill nearest to the front door.

"He's gone," she said.

My aunt was totally perplexed. "He's coming in by the back," she said, explaining that she had seen him heading for home across the fields above the house.

Taking her gently by the hands, my mother ushered her sister down to the bedroom where the others were kneeling, reciting a decade of the rosary as the spirit of the recently deceased began a different journey home.

My aunt was inconsolable according to my mother and even with the evidence of a corpse in front of her, she wanted to believe what she said she had witnessed up the field a short time earlier.

This incident only went to heighten the incredible bond between them across the great divide. From being "Daddy's girl" in life, she became "Daddy's voice" after his death and would not brook a cross word from anyone about him, particularly from her mother.

Unlike the present day when ownership of land is well documented and recorded in state offices, there was less formality about names on needs in those times.

This led to a dispute following the death of my grandfather over The Glebe and who owned it. His own family felt that it should revert to them and had begun to put stock into it as part of that process. With no man in my mother's house, my aunt, although still not a teenager, was forced to hunt the cattle that weren't hers out of the holding.

The cloak and dagger row went on with gates being opened and neighbours having to cycle into my grandmother's house to tell them that their cattle were on the road.

A resolution in the dispute came from the most unlikely of sources and certainly would never happen in the modern age.

A man who lived close by to the land had observed what was happening and one day when my aunt was down herding, saw a person from the other side of the family approach her in the middle of the field.

Immediately, he ran down the road and after listening from behind the ditch to the discourse, climbed over the gate and called out to the two to stop their squabbling.

He looked at my aunt first, then the other man and declared:

"I had to put manners on you at school 30 years ago with a few beatings and I tell you now as sure as there is a God in heaven, if you ever darken this field again, I will not be responsible for my actions. You leave this little girleen and her father's property and never cast a greedy eye in their direction again."

My aunt said it was a day that her father had worked a miracle for her. She had pains in her stomach every time she considered having to make the journey to the land and now this man who she had never spoken to previously in her life had ridden to her aid.

The man then told my aunt how he had always found her father a great and generous gentleman. The two had the same problem, he confided, but he told her that on more than one occasion her father had bailed him out of debt.

When my aunt thanked him profusely as they were parting, he turned to her with a sigh and said: "If I can do that much for him, then it is my honour and my privilege."

What was even more miraculous, my aunt would recall later, was the fact that from that day onwards she never had a moment's trouble with anyone over the land that in time she handed onto my mother after she and my father were married.

I tell the story because, when in turn my mother left the land to me, my aunt took great care to remind me of its history. She also asked that I never forget the good deed of a virtual stranger and to say a prayer for him for the way he looked after her father's interest following his death.

"It would never happen in today's world," she insisted, "but that's how the dispute over The Glebe was settled once and for all."

Sixteen

Finding A Necklace For Eternity

NO one knew her when she returned to the town she had left as a young teenager to earn money in Dublin and send back to her widowed mother.

As a spinster, she spent almost 50 years working in the Irish Hospitals' Sweepstake in the city, living in a room in her aunt's house on nearby Leeson St.

When her aunt died, the house was sold on to pay the debts that her life had incurred. The spinster felt elated when the new owner, an elderly woman, offered to rent her the top floor for a fairly nominal price.

She was my father's sister – the third child born in

a family of seven. A bookworm with an enquiring mind, she was direct in her approach to people and was devoid of guile. She couldn't mince her words on any subject and ended up only really being understood by her family and those closest to her.

She was my least favourite aunt, because she preferred my brother and my younger cousin to me. On several occasions she even had to ask me what my name was. I wasn't the only one to suffer in her judgement.

She found my father rustic in his views, her next oldest brother controversial and disagreeable and apparently it was the brother they had lost in their youth that she felt closest to in terms of family, outlook and personality.

Her father had died when she was only 10 and she had been shipped to her aunt's on his side, who was childless, to be finished off in school before being sent out to work. The cut-off from her natural family and the upheaval of effectively losing two parents at a time when only one had died, meant she went through life with a strong feeling of disconnect in terms of family closeness.

As soon as her education ended, her aunt in Dublin found suitable if low-paid employment for her where she stayed until the Sweep was founded – after that it became the only working life she ever knew. She had three weeks holidays every year, two of which she spent in our town with her sister, the youngest of their family.

She came for a week in the summer where she hid for much of the time behind the shrubs of the garden. We only knew she was there by the plume of smoke that came from the cigarettes that were perpetually between her lips.

She would then return to Dublin to her lodgings for the second week to catch a few plays or theatre events in the city.

At Christmas she came for another week. Her giftss reflected her disconnect from family life. My brother and I got aftershave lotion from the time we were 10 and before that selection boxes or obtuse books about Irish Songbirds or Parables of Saints.

On the first day of her arrival either in summer or at Christmas, my cousin, my brother and I were spruced up and told to be extra vigilant and dutiful around her by our parents. This we tried to do but she could see through pretence a mile off and would wither us with caustic comments like: "Only I've no money, I'd swear you three are acting as if you're after it."

I was afraid of her and decided the best way to deal with her was to give her a wide berth and only speak if spoken to.

My other aunt, her younger sister, was by nature nice to everyone but would feel even more empathy with someone she knew was a very lonely person. Although the subject seldom if ever came up, it was mentioned that she once had had a boyfriend, a soldier, who died in the Second World War and that ended her interest in men and a family of her own.

Mindful that she always was looking in rather than being a part of a family in these situations, my aunt would dance attention and love on her elder sister that went above and beyond the call of duty.

"You," she would say back to her. "You're too good to be true. A Pollyanna if ever there was one."

My favourite aunt would smile at such a rebuke and explain to us: "That's her way of being nice."

A funny way for sure, but if my aunt said it, I was inclined to believe her.

We would all accompany her to the railway station as she went back to Dublin in early January to be at her desk for the following day's work. We walked the half-mile, stayed on the platform for the train's arrival, and then waved her goodbye until the carriage she was in disappeared from our view.

She loved her work and you got the feeling that holidays were forced on her and she could not wait to return to the normal rhythm of life by walking from Leeson St to Ballsbridge in the morning, return for her lunch and once again at six o'clock after the day's work was completed.

She knew the important people in the 'Sweep' and the personalities which made her workplace a household name around the world in an age before national lotteries were allowed.

There was great prestige to be a worker in the

'Sweep' and when the draw was being made, it was the focus of attention in every household where a ticket had been bought.

To our surprise she arrived down for St Patrick's Day one year with her brother who lived near her in Dublin. There was a reason for her visit. She was now 65 years old and she was being retired by her employers whether she liked it or not.

Clearly she did not. Not for the first time a person who felt indispensible to an organisation had been told that her time had come. She was presented with a gold watch at a Friday evening ceremony and someone else took over her desk on the following Monday morning.

Although her pension was small, she made it clear despite constant invites from her sister that she would rather curl up and die than come down and live among us.

Her situation was compounded when the woman who owned the house she lived in on Leeson St passed away and her next of kin were eager to sell up and asked my aunt to leave.

Her sister and brother-in-law went up on the train for weeks on end in an attempt to find her alternative accommodation. Finally, they ended up renting the top half of a house from a lovely family in Dun Laoghaire.

It meant my aunt could keep most of her fine antique furniture and while it was a bit off the beaten path, it was a sunny road and she appeared to appreciate both the company and the sense of room the host family gave her in equal measure.

However, with the weight of time on her hands in retirement, she began to make excuses to come home to my aunt's house a little more than when she was working.

Although she seldom had much time to display it, she had green fingers and planted and replanted shrubs and flowerbeds across the two areas in the front of her sister's bungalow. People walking by would compliment her on how well her lilac tree was taking or how the cherry blossom was decorating the footpath with its confetti.

She took time to stand up, take the cigarette out of her mouth and even detailed her plans to do such things as move a rhododendron to the sunnier side as it would thrive better there.

In the course of her visits, I began to talk to her about the performances by Hilton Edwards and Micheál MacLiammoir that she had seen in the Gate Theatre and she would talk about the great plays she had attended at the Abbey. She would also recall the glory days of Jimmy O'Dea and Maureen Potter and how they had made Ireland laugh at dark times when people had little or nothing.

I felt a strange bond growing between us when she told me that short stories were her favourite type of literature and she had a huge 650-page collection which she offered to lend me "provided I didn't damage it and returned it in one piece."

I was at once delighted she would offer me such a personal belonging while at the same time terrified that anything would happen to it while in my possession.

Her favourite story was 'The Necklace' by French writer Guy de Maupassant. It tells the tragic tale of a young woman from the underclasses who is offered the loan of a necklace by a member of the aristocracy with whom she was friendly, to wear to a ball. After a wonderful night, she lost the diamond piece and in a panic went out and bought one with a loan that put her and her husband in debt for over a decade.

The denouement of the story came when she finally admitted to her rich friend that she had lost the necklace and then replaced it and paid it back by working long hours for many, many years. The lady is overcome but tells her lower-class friend it was an imitation piece that was worth very little.

In effect it was a story of a wasted life, or at least the best years of one and it is a story that has a particular but different meaning for every reader.

My aunt spent five years of her retirement coming and going from Dun Laoghaire but loving the seasons, particularly spring when she was at her busiest planting and sowing. Passersby continued to comment on how her work was progressing and there were moments during that communion with the earth that she seemed to find an aura and a happiness that I hadn't ever seen in her before.

The constant smoking though was having a deleterious affect on her health and she became weaker as she found it harder to eat properly.

Her sister had given her the front bedroom as her own and it was a source of comfort even in the month of May that while she couldn't tend her garden, she could see the flowers, the bushes and the shrubs as they opened up in a kaleidoscope of colour.

After prolonged fits of coughing and gasping for breath, she would lie back and her eyes would light up at the mention of the lovely fragrance wafting into the room from the outside.

Following a visit to her on one such early summer's evening when the colour had temporarily returned to her cheeks thanks to the power of what she had sown, it was a shock to be told by my uncle early next morning that she had passed away during the night.

Her sister had always insisted on closing the windows at night because she didn't want her to catch a cold.

When they found my aunt in bed the next morning, both windows were wide open and she was propped up against her pillows, her hands spread out either side of her as if she was conducting an orchestra.

For virtually all of her life she had been a slave to duty as if paying off a debt for an invisible necklace, but in death she found the moment the necklace was her own and she could wear it with pride into eternity.

Acknowledgements

I WOULD like to thank everyone who helped me in any way to make this book possible.

In particular I want to thank my daughter Rachel for her editing of the stories and perceptions as to how the content might be ordered. I would also like to thank Rosemary, my wife and Barry, my eldest son, for forensically going through the stories line by line.

I feel privileged to have grown up within such a community in Clara where the richness of loyalty and fun sustained a generation, often against the odds.

Lastly I would like to honour the memory of Mary Keane, widow of John B, who passed away this year and whose encouragement meant so much to me down through the years.

Also By Ballpoint Press

Around The Farm Gate

With contributions from

Margaret Bourke – *The Last Of The Country Cures*

Nora Brennan – *A Day In The Drills*

Noreen Brennan-Donoghue – *A Turf-Saving Deliverance*

Pauline Brew – *The Milking Parlour*

Mary Buckley – *Killing The Pig*

Jack Byrne – *The Vixen And The Pup*

Tom Byrne – *The Best Wheat In The Barrow Valley*

Eileen Casey – *The Quiet Man*

Helen Calvey – *The Day The Banshee Was Heard On Achill Island*

Mary Conliffe – *The Bogeyman In The Barn*

Sandra Coffey – *The Cows' Highway*

Ciaran Condren – *The Race To The Bottom Of The World*

Declan Coyle – *Crossing The Great Divide*

Joe Coyle – *The Mice In The Meadow*

Edward Cunningham – *Horsemen Passing By*

Brigid Daly – *Rural Slices*

Dan Daly – *The Threshing*

John Dillion – *The Murhur Reel*

Maeve Edwards – *The Long Grass*

Patricia Finn – *The Cockerel*

Mike Flahive – *Cows At The Cliffside*

Bunty Flynn – *A Quiet Christmas*

Johnny Flynn – *The Maypole*

Moira Gallagher – *The Potato Sowers*

Declan P Gowran – *Scythe Man*

Seán Hallinan – *The White Face*

James Keane – *Cuckoo Oats and Woodcock Hay*

Joe Keane – *Seasons in Scenes And Sounds*

Joe Kearney – *A Spot Of Dust*

Daniel Kearns – *The Big Chill of 1947*

Robert Leonard – *The Great Turnip Swindle of 1955*

Eileen Ludlow – *The Secret Killer*

Michael Lynch – *The Country Shop*

Tony McCormack – *A Love Story Of The Mountains*

Mark McGaugh – *The First Ploughing Day Of Spring*

Jim McNamara – *Taming Sally*

Christopher Moore – *Milk Cheque Joy*

Patsy O'Brien – *The King Of The Road*

Mary O'Connor – *The Spailpín*

Patrick O'Dwyer – *The Cow That Went On Holidays*

Denis O'Higgins – *The White Cow Whinger*

Gearóid Ó Ciaráin – *Fair Day In Kildysart*

Art Ó Suilleabháin – *Majesty Of The Kestrels*

Vincet Power – *A Day In The Life Of A Farm*

Catherine Power-Evans – *Maps, Gaps and Patchwork Fields*

Tom Rowley – *The Bend At The Church*

Lorna Sixsmith – *Stranger On The Floor*

Rhoda Twombly – *The Lion In The Lamb*

Gretta Tynan – *Achtung... Lights, Camera And Action*

Meta Waters – *The Night Liston KO'd Patterson And My Mother*

'Around The Farm Gate' is a collaborative project between RTÉ Radio 1, the *Irish Farmers Journal* and Ballpoint Press Limited.